W9-ACU-942

DATE DUE

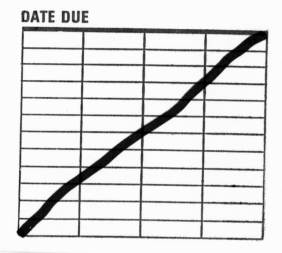

UGANDA

TRUDY J. HANMER

FRANKLIN WATTS
NEW YORK • LONDON
TORONTO • SYDNEY • 1989
A VENTURE BOOK

Library of Congress Cataloging-in-Publication Data

Hanmer, Trudy J.
Uganda / Trudy J. Hanmer.
p.   cm.—(A Venture book)
Includes index.
Summary: Discusses the history, culture, and people of Uganda.
ISBN 0-531-10816-3
1. Uganda—Juvenile literature.   [1. Uganda.]   I. Title.
DT433.222.H36   1989
967.6'1—dc19   89-31171   CIP   AC

For Maisie and Pip

Maps by Joe Le Monnier

Photographs courtesy of
Magnum: pp. 19 (Chris Steele-Perkins),
21 and 70 (George Rodger), 99 (Abbas),
111 and 119 (Chris Steele-Perkins);
East African Office: p. 24; New York
Public Library Picture Collection:
pp. 40, 54; Culver Pictures: pp. 43,
45, 64, 67; Pictorial Parade: p. 88,
90, 93, 96, 102; Reuters/Bettmann
Newsphotos: p. 116.

CONTENTS

Introduction
11

Chapter One
"Pearl of Africa"
15

Chapter Two
The People of Uganda
31

Chapter Three
Buganda and the British
47

Chapter Four
Uganda as a British Protectorate
63

Chapter Five
Uganda Returns to Independence
82

Chapter Six
Uganda in the 1980s
109

Glossary 123
Index 125

UGANDA

INTRODUCTION

For generations, the *Baganda* people of Uganda
have recited an old legend that explains how
death was introduced to earth. According to the
legend, many thousands of years ago a man
named Kintu owned a single cow. When Kintu's
cow was stolen, he went to Heaven to get it
back. (In the legend, Heaven takes the form of
a person.) When Kintu asked Heaven about his
cow, Heaven declared that not until Kintu broke
a mountain of rock and ate a mountain of food
would his cow be returned to him. When Kintu
had completed these tasks, his cow was returned, and Kintu prepared to go home.

While visiting Heaven, however, Kintu had fallen in love with Nambi, Heaven's daughter, and he asked her to return to earth with him. Nambi agreed; but halfway there, she ran back to her home to get food for her pet chicken. Kintu did not want Nambi to risk going back, for he feared that she would be detained by her brother, Walumbi, who was also known as Death. Although Walumbi did not capture Nambi, he did follow her and Kintu to earth. In this way, Death came to the world.

This legend is an important one because the history of Uganda, a country long dominated economically by the Baganda, is a sad one. Death has stalked Uganda for many centuries in the form of disease and warfare. In the past, Uganda has been the site of terrible epidemics of sleeping sickness. Today, its people face a spreading epidemic of AIDS. Before Europeans came to Africa, the peoples who make up modern Uganda had been divided for centuries by violent civil fighting. Foreigners introduced Islam and Christianity by the nineteenth century; religious differences added new causes for war.

The devastation of Uganda and the death of Uganda's people are especially ironic and tragic because the area occupied by modern Uganda contains some of the richest land in Africa. Unlike many African nations where people starve and die because of drought and famine, Uganda is agriculturally rich. Except in a few areas of the country, Ugandans have no difficulty growing enough food to eat.

There is another reason why the violence of modern Uganda is ironic. When Europeans penetrated the interior of the African continent in the middle of the nineteenth century, the tribal kingdoms they encountered in Buganda and Bunyoro were models of efficient bureaucracy and sophisticated political organization. The system of shared responsibility among monarch, ministers, and legislators seemed familiar to the outsiders, especially the British, who were used to a king and queen, a prime minister, and a parliament. For a time, it appeared that these similarities would make Uganda's transition to a modern nation—the seemingly inevitable result of European exploration—smoother than that transition had been for nations whose political and social systems were less familiar to the British. Yet, too often in the twentieth century, Uganda's modern leaders have kept the violence and autocracy of their ancestors and have ignored their traditions of shared power and service to their people.

After he had seen Uganda, Winston Churchill, a man who had seen much of the world, wrote, "Uganda is a fairy tale. You climb up a railway instead of a beanstalk, and at the top there is a wonderful new world." The history of Uganda shares a lot with fairy tales—kings and princesses, exotic animals, brave adventurers, giant plants, and colorful birds. But Uganda, like fairy tales, also has monsters and villains and surprise events that destroy and kill. Sadly for Uganda, the bad things are all too real, and there is as yet no good fairy who can wave her magic wand and make the evil go away.

"PEARL OF AFRICA"

Winston Churchill nicknamed the Kingdom of Uganda the "pearl of Africa," for so it seemed to him and to other British adventurers and conquerors at the beginning of the twentieth century. Everything about Uganda made it a rich and valuable part of the British Empire. The British believed that the societies around Lake Victoria could very quickly be made into the modern nation of Uganda.

Uganda is one of three nations that are part of the area of Africa known as East Africa. The other two countries are Kenya and Tanzania (once divided into Tanganyika and Zanzibar).

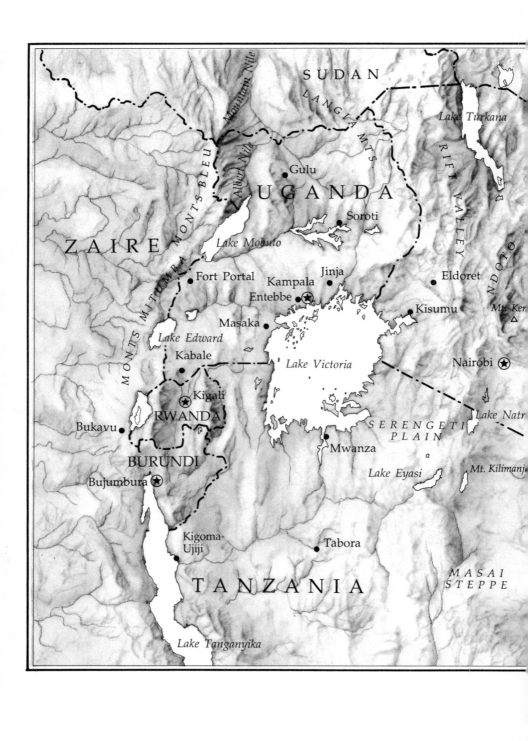

These nations share certain geographic features that make it logical and convenient for historians and people outside the area to think of them as one area. To the north, they are bounded by the mountains of Sudan and the deserts of Somali. On the west, they are bordered by a string of lakes, from Lake Albert in the north to Lake Tanganyika in the south. The borders of Tanzania, Rwanda, and Zaire delineate their southern boundary, and the eastern border of the region is formed by the Indian Ocean.

Uganda is a tiny nation, comparable in size to the state of Oregon. Uganda covers 91,134 square miles (236,036 sq km). The country is landlocked, which means that it has no direct access to ocean ports. Uganda's neighbor on the north is Sudan; on the west, Zaire; on the south, Rwanda and Tanzania; and on the east, Kenya.

In the mid-1980s, the population of Uganda was estimated to be slightly over 15 million people. Ninety percent of Uganda's people are agricultural workers, and fewer than 10 percent of them live in urban areas. Uganda's major city is Kampala, the capital. Slightly more than half of Uganda's people can read and write.

A study in contrast: the lushly green countryside of Uganda; in the background, its modern capital, Kampala

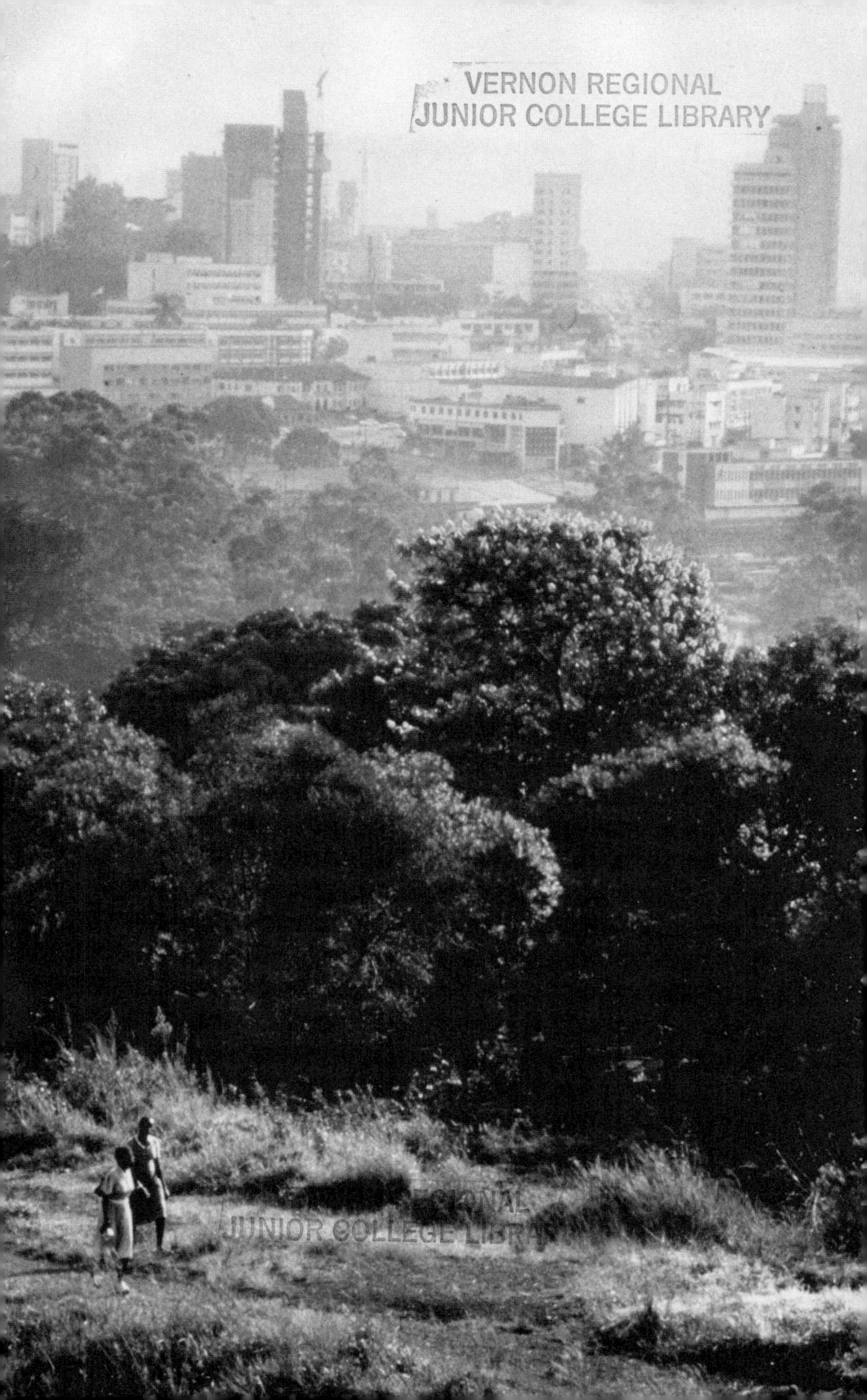

Life expectancy in Uganda is not high. Not only do the people of Uganda suffer from poor health, but in recent years terrible wars and civil unrest have cost the lives of thousands of Ugandans. The average Ugandan male can expect to live to be forty-nine and the average Ugandan female to be fifty-three. (In the Soviet Union, by comparison, the average male life expectancy is sixty-two and female is seventy-three. In the United States, men can expect to live seventy-two years and women seventy-nine years.)

Infant mortality in Uganda is extremely high. Out of every 1,000 babies born, 113 will die. (This compares with 10 in the United States and 31 in the Soviet Union.) Medical care is very inadequate. In the late 1980s, there were only about 650 doctors practicing in Uganda.

Uganda's current form of government is a military dictatorship. Uganda has a president, a prime minister, a legislature, and a court system. The country is organized into ten provinces and thirty-four districts. For the last quarter of a century, elections have been held erratically, and most changes in government have been accompanied by bloodshed and violence.

Some of the tensions within the country are religious. Uganda is 63 percent Christian and 10 percent Moslem, while the rest of the people follow indigenous religions. Other internal divisions stem from regional, class, and economic conflicts. The four major language divisions in

A schoolboy in the Ugandan province of Bunyoro
writes, with his teacher's direction,
a sentence in English on the chalkboard.

the country are Bantu, Nilotic, Nilo-Hamitic, and Sudanic. English and *Swahili* are both designated as official languages, but Swahili is spoken by most of the people to transact everyday business.

Throughout the 681,189 square miles (1,764,516 sq km) that compose East Africa, the most striking physical characteristic is the *rift valleys*. These are especially prominent in Uganda. Much of the land surface of Uganda, particularly its plateaus and lakes, was created when the earth was being formed and great rock shelves beneath the earth's surface folded back on themselves.

Although the first "rifting," as this geological phenomenon is called, took place millions of years ago during the period known as pre-Cambrian, much of the great rift valley in Uganda was formed during more recent times, probably after people were living in the area. In most other places in the world, the earth took the shape it has now—mountains, lakes, deserts, forests—before people appeared.

Because of the rift valleys, modern Uganda is a land of plateaus and deep basins. Most of the basins are filled with beautiful lakes. The largest is Lake Victoria, which is the third largest freshwater lake in the world. Other important lakes filling the depressions in Uganda's plateaus are Lake Albert, Lake George, and Lake Edward. All of these lakes lie well above sea level. For centuries, people have been attracted to their shores, not only because the lakes provide a water supply but also because of their pleasant climate. Because of their location well above sea level, the climate around them is not nearly as hot and tropical as we would normally expect to find in latitudes so close to the equator. The surface of Lake Victoria, for example, is nearly 4,000 feet (1,219 m) above sea level. The most prosperous early peoples settled along the shores of this lake, and the present capital city of Kampala is located on Victoria's northern shore.

Although nearly all of Uganda is at least 3,000 feet (914 m) or more above sea level, along the border with Zaire, the land soars even higher. Here are located the fabled Mountains of the Moon that have fascinated geographers, mapmakers, and explorers for many centuries.

More properly called the Ruwenzori Mountains (*Ruwenzori* is a Swahili term for rainmaker), these tall mountains play an important role in keeping Uganda's agriculture so productive. Although the Ruwenzori Mountains are located almost on the equator, they help stimulate regular rainfall so that Uganda, unlike many African nations, has never had to worry about drought. These mountains have also been important in protecting Uganda from invasion from the west. The Ruwenzori range is 60 miles long and 30 miles across (97 km; 48.5 km), a formidable obstacle for enemies to penetrate.

*The Ruwenzori Mountains, with their giant lobelias,
heathers, and far views of glaciers and peaks*

The Ruwenzori may have been first called Mountains of the Moon by early Egyptian scientists. Over thirty-nine hundred years ago, they wrote of the Lunae Montes (Latin for *lunar*, or *moon*, mountains) of Central Africa. Fourteen hundred years later, the Greek dramatist Aeschylus suggested that the Nile River, the greatest river then known to the Greeks, was "fed by distant snow" in the Ruwenzori. The search for the source of the Nile led many Egyptians, Greeks, and Europeans over the centuries to speculate on the great mountains rising in the African interior. Until the last two hundred years, few of these outsiders had actually explored the area. Even with today's modern equipment and technology, climbing the Ruwenzori is a tricky and hazardous business.

A major reason for this difficulty is that these mountains rise into the clouds and seem to disappear—reach to the moon. For three hundred days of the year, the tops of the mountains are invisible to people in the valleys below. Lost in the clouds, the peaks seem shrouded in mystery. The highest of these are well over 16,000 feet (4,843 m) so that there is always snow on top of the mountains in spite of their location 30 miles (48.5 km) north of the equator. The highest peaks are Mount Margherita, 16,763 feet (5,111 m), Mount Alexandra, 16,750 feet (5,109 m), and Mount Baker, 16,040 feet (4,830 m).

In addition to the Ruwenzori, Uganda has one other area of high elevation—the volcanic mountains known as the Mufumbiro volcanoes. Most of the Mufumbiro are located along the borders that Uganda shares with Zaire and Rwanda. The highest of these is Muhavura. Some of the Mufumbiro are still active; throughout this area are valleys that have extremely rich soils from the Mufumbiro lava.

The mountainous areas of Uganda are the source of most of Uganda's mineral resources. Iron ore, copper, and cobalt are abundant, but mining to develop these resources has been interrupted by the political and economic chaos of recent years. The mountains with their lakes and rivers also provide sources for hydroelectric power.

The presence of mountains and plateaus, the major characteristics of the rift valley, determines the climate of Uganda. Uganda has a warm, not hot, climate. Many African nations suffer from lack of rainfall because the air temperature close to the equator causes the earth's surface water to evaporate far more rapidly than rainfall can replace it. Even Uganda's East African neighbors, Kenya and Tanzania, suffer from droughts more often than Uganda does.

Uganda, however, is specially favored by nature. Most of the country receives over 40 inches (100 cm) of rainfall per year. In the highlands, the average temperature falls in the 60s°F (16–18°C), and in Kampala, the average high temperature falls around 80°F (27°C). Compared to the average temperatures of other African capitals, this is quite comfortable. In the Ruwenzori, of course, the temperatures are very cold. Because of these cold temperatures near the equator, the ice and snow melt and refreeze continually. The effect of this is to create lacy patterns in the ice on the mountains and icicles that are often over 10 feet (3 m) long.

The few locations in Uganda that do not have regular, steady annual rainfall are poorer areas that have not shared the prosperity of Uganda, even in good times. These areas are generally located in the northern and western parts of the country, in the provinces of Ankole, Masaka, Bukoba, and Karageve. In the east, the Karamoja district bordering on Kenya is a particularly dry area.

Uganda is renowned for the variety and quantity of its animal life. On the slopes of the Ruwenzori live some of the most exotic animals in the world. The rock hyrax, a rabbit with hooves that is a zoological relative of the elephant and the rhinoceros, makes its home here. So do earthworms that grow to be 3 feet (0.9 m) long.

In the rolling plains of the grassy savanna in the north live over forty species of large mammals, for example, elephants, buffaloes, lions, leopards, zebras, and giraffes. Uganda is also the home of the largest and smallest of the African primates: the giant gorillas and the tiny galago, or "bush baby," with its owl eyes and flat nails.

On the golf course in Kampala, there is a special rule. If a golf ball lands in the pawprint of a hippopotamus, the golfer is allowed to move the ball, without penalty, to a flat area. Hippo prints are so deep that to have to loft a golf ball out of one is considered unfair. And hippo prints are so common that the ground rule has been part of the course rules for nearly a century.

Hippopotamuses, gazelles, hartebeest, oribi, crocodiles, eland, topi, bushbuck, and antelopes share the Uganda rain forests and plains with a number of exotic birds. Ostriches, kites, and fish eagles—sharp-eyed birds that can swoop down without warning on a fish they have spotted over half a mile away—fill the skies and live along the lake shores.

One of the smallest animals in Uganda, an insect, has had the greatest influence on the lives of the people and other mammals living in this area. The *tsetse fly* (officially known by its Latin name, *Glossina*) carries a variety of diseases that have plagued Ugandans and killed their cattle for centuries. As much as one-third of the country of Uganda has been infested with the tsetse fly. Ironically, the fly thrives in the lake area where most people live and most agriculture is done.

The disease carried by the tsetse fly is generally called "sleeping sickness." When this disease occurs in humans, it is usually fatal. The medical name for this disease in humans is *trypanosomiasis*, and in cattle and other animals it is nagana. In both humans and in cattle, this is a serious, deadly disease. When cattle are infected, humans cannot use their meat or milk. During the early years of the twentieth century, a terrible epidemic of sleeping sickness struck Uganda. Of the three hundred thousand people living in the immediate area of the epidemic, two hundred thousand died.

Although Uganda is an agriculturally rich country, Ugandans do not grow a great variety of crops. For many centuries, the banana has provided the staple for the Ugandan diet. In addition, Ugandans grow finger millet, cassava, sorghum, maize, sweet potatoes, groundnuts, sesame, and beans. Coffee and cotton have been grown for export since the beginning of this century.

Sorghum, millet, and groundnuts have been grown in East Africa ever since people there began to practice agriculture. The banana, or plantain, was probably introduced to the area by voyagers who crossed the Indian Ocean from India or Malaysia and brought this crop with them. Other staple crops—principally, maize, cassava, and sweet potatoes—were brought to Africa by Europeans. Often those Europeans "discovered" these crops in the Western Hemisphere. Europeans, especially Englishmen, who colonized Uganda in the late nineteenth century, were responsible for agricultural experiments that spread the use of these crops. They were also responsible for stimulating the growth of coffee and cotton as cash crops.

The wild vegetation of Uganda ranges from savanna grasses to tropical rain forests. The savanna is most prevalent. On the shores of the lakes, reeds and papyrus plants are common. Most of the plants native to Uganda are tropical or semitropical.

The comfortable climate, the spectacular scenery, the wildlife, and the lush plant life made the lake country of East Africa a highly populous area. These factors also contributed to the area's attractiveness to the Europeans who tried to make the peoples of Uganda recognize and live within a modern nationalistic structure.

THE PEOPLE
OF UGANDA

The word *Uganda* is Swahili for "land of the Ganda," but the Ganda, although they have been the dominant people of this area, are only one group among the many who call themselves Ugandans. The Bantu word for the area around Lake Victoria, the area of the Ganda kingdom, is *Buganda*. The words *Ganda* and *Baganda* are interchangeable and refer to the people of Buganda. Often the word *Ugandan* is used to mean Baganda or Ganda. In the Ganda language, known as *Luganda*, a single member of the tribe is a *Muganda*. For as long as there has been recorded history and for many centuries before,

Uganda has been a land of diverse people and culture.

For many years, anthropologists believed that the earliest evidence of people on earth had been found on the continent of Asia. More recently, scientists have focused on the remains of the ancient people they have found in the African continent, particularly in and near Uganda. What these people were like, how they looked, or how they lived is very difficult to determine.

The first Ugandans about whom anthropologists can answer these questions lived thousands of years ago during the Stone Age. Stone Age tools, specifically Kafuan pebble tools, have been discovered along the western shore of Lake Victoria, evidence that a well-developed Stone Age culture existed in this area. Because these artifacts have been found in the area of Sango Bay, the culture they represent has been called the Sangoan culture.

The Stone Age culture lasted in Uganda until about fifty thousand years ago. The use of pebble tools was followed by the development of hand axes. After that, some people learned to use wood and leather to make more sophisticated stone tools. The people who used these tools were hunters and nomads who wandered from place to place; they had not yet learned about cultivating the land. The two major groups of these people were called Bushmen and Proto-

Hamites. Although these people must have been the ancestors of the current Ugandans, they lived so long ago that it is impossible to trace which habits and customs they may have passed down to their modern descendants. It is possible, however, to trace the roots of modern Ugandans to the people who inhabited the region from the sixteenth century on.

In modern Uganda, the descendants of the ancient Ugandans are organized into ten major tribes and a host of smaller ones. A tribe by definition is a group of people who share a common language, a common land ownership, and a sense that any outsiders who do not belong to the tribe are at worst, enemies, or at best, strangers. For centuries, tribal membership and regionalism have provided the people in this area with a sense of identity. Unfortunately, during modern times, strong tribal feelings have also been the cause of much of the internal tension in Uganda.

The most common individual tribes in Uganda today can be organized according to four language groups. Although tribes within a language group may speak in their own dialects—special words, phrases, or accents that belong solely to that tribe—in general, they speak the same major language. Each of the four major language groups dominates a specific area of Uganda. In the south, the *Bantu* predominates;

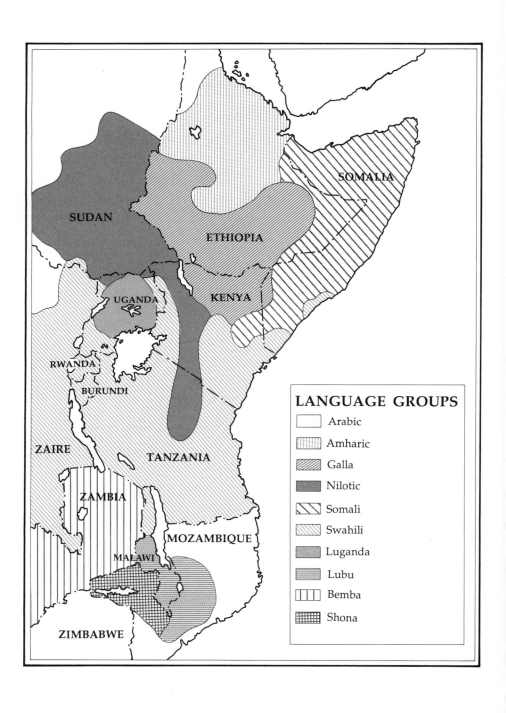

LANGUAGE GROUPS

	Arabic
	Amharic
	Galla
	Nilotic
	Somali
	Swahili
	Luganda
	Lubu
	Bemba
	Shona

SUDAN

SOMALIA

ETHIOPIA

KENYA

UGANDA

RWANDA

BURUNDI

ZAIRE

TANZANIA

ZAMBIA

MOZAMBIQUE

MALAWI

ZIMBABWE

in the north central, the *Nilotic;* in the northwest, the *Sudanese;* and in the northeast, the *Nilo-Hamitic.*

The Bantu are the most numerous by far. Their major tribe is the Ganda, but the Bantu also include the Gisa, the Soga, the Nyoro, the Nkole, and the Toro. The major Nilotic tribes include the Acholi, the Alur, the Kakwa, and the Langi. The three major Sudanese tribes are the Lugbara, the Madi, and the Logo; and the Nilo-Hamitic include the Iteso, the *Karamojong,* and the Sebei.

By the time that Europeans invaded Africa in the nineteenth century and began to write about the people they encountered there, the Bantu tribes, especially the Ganda and the Nyoro, dominated the region that would become modern Uganda. The Ganda maintained their position of supremacy throughout most of the last century. However, the Ganda did not always play such a large role in this area. Over time, the migration into and out of Uganda by many different tribes and the warfare among them eventually left the Ganda in a position of power.

As far as historians can tell, the center of the Bantu culture in the eighth and ninth centuries was the Luba-Lunda region in what is now Zaire. Here the Bantu developed a sophisticated civilization using copper as their main metal. They had also entered the Iron Age and were able to fashion tools from this metal.

Betwen A.D. 500 and 1000, the Bantu began to spread east to Lake Victoria. They had become an agricultural people and were attracted to the rich soils in the area. With them, they brought the banana and so are credited with introducing this vital crop to the country. The Soga and the Ganda were among the Bantu tribes living in what is now southern Uganda by the end of the fifteenth century A.D.

During the first five centuries that the Bantu inhabited the shores of Lake Victoria, they were frequently at war with other tribes. For a time, they were dominated by the Hima and the Tutsi, warrior tribes from the west. Then, sometime during the fifteenth and sixteenth centuries, Nilotic immigrants from the north, chiefly the *Lwo* (ancestors of the Acholi and the Langi tribes) traveled through what are now the northern districts of Uganda to reach the shores of Lake Victoria.

The Bantu culture that the Lwo encountered was far more well developed than their own nomadic, wandering culture. The Bantu, especially the Ganda, included prosperous farmers. The Nilotic peoples depended heavily on cattle, both as a sign of wealth and for food. However, little of that early Bantu culture survived the onslaught of the Lwo, so the tribal culture that the Europeans first encountered truly stemmed from the blending of the tradition of the pre-1500s Bantu group and the invading Lwo. Bantu legends, including those about Kintu, the man who helped bring Death to earth, are all that is left of the earlier period.

The Bantu Kingdom that the Lwo invaded was called *Kitara*. As the Nilotic Lwo moved into Kitara, some of the people there moved west to the present-day district of Ankole. In the north-western regions of Uganda, the Nilotic invaders met with Sudanic tribes that are the forebears of the Alur and the Acholi.

Around the northern shores of Lake Victoria, a Nilotic tribe, the Bito, mixed with the Bantu to form three separate kingdoms: Bunyoro, Buganda, and Busoga. For a time, *Bunyoro* would be the most powerful of the new kingdoms. In the Bantu language, the prefix *Bu* means "land of." *Buganda* is Bantu for "land of the Ganda," just as *Uganda* is the Swahili for this same designation. The use of these two terms to describe this entire area demonstrates how important and powerful the Ganda had become.

Between the sixteenth and nineteenth centuries, power gradually shifted from Bunyoro to Buganda, both of which were well-organized kingdoms. Mutesa II, the last king to rule Buganda actively, was able to trace his ancestry to the Baganda kings of the sixteenth century. For this reason, historians date Uganda's modern history from the development of the Bantu kingdoms in the sixteenth century.

Before the coming of the Lwo, the Bantu were loosely organized according to tribal connections. With the establishment of the new kingdoms, loyalty to the monarch—a central, powerful figure—became the most important connection for the members of the tribe. All of the new Bantu kingdoms, which included the smaller kingdoms of Buddu and Buruli, as well as the larger Bunyoro and Buganda monarchies, shared certain ideas about monarchy that made the king—or *kabaka*, as he was called in Bantu—an extraordinarily powerful figure.

For many generations, Bantu tribes had been divided into clans (extended families). The new kabakas and other tribal rulers were not identified with any single clan, so they represented the tribe as a whole. The kabaka was believed to have divine power, but his rule on earth was based on the very pragmatic principle of political patronage. (Political patronage is the right of a leader, in this case the kabaka, to hand out offices to his supporters.)

Under the new Bantu kabakas, the position of chief of the clan became the gift of the king. Chiefs no longer inherited their chiefdoms. Instead they were appointed by the kabaka and installed in their new office in an elaborate ceremony. In this way, the kabaka reinforced the idea of his power and the grandeur of his office, and enlisted the absolute loyalty of the new chief. During the sixteenth and seventeenth centuries, the kabaka moved his royal court from one location to another as yet another indication that he was the king of all the people.

During the eighteenth century, the kabaka of Buganda became more and more powerful. A major reason for his power was the presence of a highly trained, highly loyal bodyguard that became the core of an army that helped Buganda expand its territory. By 1850, Buganda stretched over the entire northwestern shore of Lake Victoria, from the Nile to the Kagera River. Buganda surpassed Bunyoro in land and wealth. The ideas of a strong central government—as represented by the kabaka—and economic growth based on territorial expansion were firmly established, important principles in Buganda.

The elite corps of guards that surrounded the kabaka by the middle of the nineteenth century was well equipped with modern guns that they had learned to use most efficiently to fight any challenge to the king's authority. These guns had come from traders from the east, most often those sent by the sultan of Zanzibar. Beginning in the 1840s, Zanzibari traders had reached the shores of Lake Victoria. They sought ivory and slaves. In return, they left the Ganda with gunpowder and a new religion, Islam. Both would prove to be explosive forces in modern Uganda.

In 1852, a typical Zanzibari caravan made the slow, dangerous overland trek from the east

In the nineteenth century, Zanzibari slave traders
regularly penetrated into Uganda to buy slaves
from the kabaka in exchange for guns and
ammunition. These Zanzibari traders left in
their wake a new religion, Islam.

to lake Victoria. The expedition was led by the Snay bia Amin, an Arab who left a written record of his transactions with the kabaka. Snay bia Amin wanted slaves. He traded with the kabaka, who was all too willing to sell his enemies to the Arab. The price for an adult male was two muskets, and for a female, one hundred bullets.

Over the next decade, the Arab traders gained greater and greater influence over Buganda. Unlike later European explorers from England and France, the Arabs intermarried with the natives, spreading their influence at the clan level. Many Arabs helped convert the Baganda to Islam. Their influence was so powerful that *Mutesa I*, the kabaka at mid-century, temporarily ordered all of his subjects to worship Mohammed. In fact, it was Mutesa's fear of the growing power of the Arab traders in his kingdom that later led him to encourage British Christian missionaries to come to Buganda. Mutesa wanted their help in expelling the Arabs who, he feared, would soon take over his country.

The first British explorer to reach Buganda was John Speke, who arrived in the kingdom in 1862. What Speke found was a highly centralized, efficiently run kingdom of one million people, stretching along the northwestern shore of Lake Victoria. In addition to ruling Buganda, the kabaka controlled one million other people in the neighboring kingdoms of Soga and Haya, whose lesser kabakas paid taxes to the powerful Mutesa I of Buganda.

Mutesa I reigned from 1854 to 1884. Although Speke found Mutesa to be an extraordinarily cruel ruler by nineteenth-century British standards, the general outline of Mutesa's government was very familiar to British citizens of the Victorian era.

In addition to the kabaka, there were several other well-established members of the royal family and court. The dowager queen, or *namasole*; the queen-sister, or *lubuga*; the prime minister, or *katikiro*; were all members of the kabaka's court. There was a chief field marshal, or *mujasi*, to lead the army, and the *gabunga* served as the lord high admiral. The *mukajunga* was the lord high executioner.

This last office was extremely important in a country where death was the punishment for a great number of major and minor crimes. When Mutesa ascended the throne, he ordered all of his brothers to be put to death. This was a Ganda custom and was believed to be a way of establishing stability for the new government. The chiefs belonged to a council, or parliament, called the *lukiko*, which voted for a new kabaka from among the old kabaka's sons. By putting all the losers to death, the new kabaka ensured that no royal brother could challenge his authority. In addition to killing his brothers when he ascended the throne, Mutesa ordered that hundreds of slaves be put to death as a way of celebrating his power.

Mutesa I was remembered by Europeans who witnessed his reign as an extremely cruel ruler. In this early print, victims are being sacrificed in honor of the visit of a foreign dignitary to Mutesa's court.

The power of the kabaka was supreme. In his presence, his subjects had to keep their legs covered or suffer death, usually by being thrown to crocodiles. All of the kabaka's subjects had to throw themselves face down in the dirt when he appeared. For wearing a leopard skin (a fur that was to be worn only by royalty), a Muganda could be roasted alive over a slow fire.

The kabaka lived in a palace, and his subjects lived in sturdy, beehive-shaped bungalows made of woven reeds and tree limbs. The huts were airy and roomy and typically covered 50 square feet (4.5 sq m). To the British, these huts seemed far superior to those they had encountered while visiting other tribes who used mud and manure to build their homes. Around royal residences in Buganda, the people had built fences of elephant grass or bamboo. Separate lavatories were common.

The nineteenth-century kabaka had as many as three hundred wives living in or near the royal palace. Most women in the kingdom were the cultivators. In such a rich land, farming required little skill and was thus defined as women's work because women were believed to be far less important than men.

The nineteenth-century inhabitants of Buganda, unlike many of the tribes in the northern areas, for example the Karamojong, wore clothes. They hammered the bark of the fig tree until it was pliable and looked to Europeans like

*The capital of Mutesa I, as depicted
in the* Columbian Atlas *of 1893*

corduroy and felt like silk. The kabaka and other royalty also wore fur.

When the Arabs introduced Islam to Buganda, the predominant religion was *lubareism*, a tribal religion that called for human sacrifice as a way of appeasing and pleasing the gods. Music was an important part of both religious and royal ceremonies. The music of Buganda was complex and included the full range of sounds that might have been known to Bach. In addition to horns and drums, the Ganda musicians used harps, flutes, and xylophones.

The civilization of Buganda that John Hanning Speke encountered was highly developed. The British initially felt no need to include Buganda formally in their growing empire. It was a landlocked nation, and the nineteenth-century British were seafarers above all. As the nineteenth century wore on, however, the events of world politics would draw British attention to Buganda and lead the foreigners to believe that this small kingdom could be easily added to the British Empire. By doing so, the British believed, they could maintain a balance of power in Africa and check the French, Belgians, and Portuguese, who had also laid claim to areas of the continent.

BUGANDA AND
THE BRITISH

When John Hanning Speke reached Lake Victoria, he met formally with Mutesa I. Nearly forty years later, Mutesa's son, Mwanga, would lose Buganda and the surrounding kingdoms to the British when Uganda was absorbed by the vast nineteenth-century British Empire. Contact with Europeans, especially the British, would change Uganda forever. Using Buganda as their base, the British would create the modern state of Uganda, incorporating into it not only the four kingdoms of the lake country but also a number of diverse, warring tribes from the north.

Outlining Uganda's borders on paper and having other Europeans recognize the establishment of the area as a nation could not override the tribal animosities of generations. The British believed they could overcome this with a strong colonial government working in concert with the Baganda. The British were mistaken, but it would take most of the twentieth century for people to realize how wrong they were.

When Speke entered Buganda, he was searching for the source of the great Nile River. The interior of Africa was a vast unknown territory to Europeans in the middle of the nineteenth century. England was a rapidly industrializing nation, and the British government believed it was their duty to spread the principles of their industrialized nation to all parts of the world. They were amazingly successful at doing this; by the middle of the nineteenth century, the interior of Africa was one of the few places as yet untouched by the British.

In return for spreading industrialism and Christianity to parts of the world that knew about neither, the British got sources of raw materials, markets for their manufactured goods, and strategic locations for their navy and, occasionally, their army, to defend the Empire. In order to add the interior of Africa to the Empire, the British first had to know what was there. This was the mission for men like Richard Burton, Speke, David Livingstone, and Henry Morton Stanley, all of whom spent years traveling through parts of the African interior where no white men had been seen before.

By the time Speke made his journey to Buganda, the British had developed a strong interest in learning where the Nile River began. They controlled a corrupt monarchy in Egypt, strategically important to their navy and trade in the Mediterranean, and they wanted to protect southern access to Egypt.

John Speke had traveled through the lake country of East Africa, from the Indian Ocean to Lake Tanganyika and then north to Lake Victoria, in the late 1850s. As a result of that expedition, he surmised that Lake Victoria was the source of the Nile River. During the middle 1850s, another British explorer named David Livingstone had traveled across Africa from the Atlantic Ocean to the Indian Ocean and had reported on his travels to the Royal Geographical Society in London. Fascinated by Livingstone's tales and interested in testing Speke's theory about the Nile, the Royal Geographical Society paid Speke to return to Africa. The idea was so popular that the British public raised money to help with the expedition, and the British government also contributed to the cause.

Speke left England in 1860 and arrived in Buganda in January 1862. After exploring the area, he came to the incorrect conclusion that his original hypothesis was right: the Nile began in Lake Victoria. Speke reported to England two things: his geographic finding and his belief that Buganda provided the perfect setting for Protestant missionaries from Great Britain to spread Christianity to the interior of Africa. Fortunately for the continued peace of Buganda, the few British missionaries along the coast of Africa were having a difficult enough time spreading the gospel to the people there. The idea of trekking into the interior to live out of communication with the British navy was not at all appealing. For the next twelve years, no further British visitors went to Buganda.

During the period, other foreigners continued to trade with Buganda and in some cases expressed an interest in taking over the kingdom. The Zanzibari slave traders maintained their terrible business of capturing and selling Africans in return for guns. These traders, who had been engaged in the slave trade in Uganda for over twenty years, had well-established trading posts all along the route from the Indian Ocean to Lake Victoria. Periodically, Mutesa would expel them from his kingdom when he felt they were growing too powerful. His opinion of Islam changed back and forth. Like his father, Suna, before him, he was intrigued by the new religion. However, he was also wary of its impact on his people.

Lubareism, the religion of Buganda, was a casual religion, apparently in evidence most often on special occasions. There was no one god to threaten the supreme position of the earthly ruler, the kabaka. Mutesa was an intelligent man, and his intellectual curiosity led him to learn as much as he could about Islam (and later about Christianity). At the same time, he was shrewd and jealous of his power. He recognized that Islam gave his people someone new—Allah and Mohammed—to worship above their kabaka. He felt he could not afford this threat to his power.

Mutesa was forced to ally himself with the Zanzibari traders, however, because a more immediate threat to his power emerged in the 1860s and remained a constant worry until the arrival of more British in the 1870s. Mutesa was worried about an Egyptian invasion of his kingdom.

Egypt in the 1860s was ruled by the Khedive Ismail, who controlled Egypt for Turkey. The khedive worried about growing British power in the Mediterranean. He wanted to stay on their good side, and he wanted to increase Egypt's territory. He thought he had a plan that would do both.

In 1869, Khedive Ismail hired the British explorer Samuel Baker to be the "Governor General of the Equatorial Nile Basin." Baker had written a best-selling book about his African travels, *The Albert Nyanza*, which had aroused British public opinion against the horrors of the Nile slave trade. Slavery had been outlawed in Great Britain in 1833. Most Europeans viewed the Nile slave trade as proof of the barbarism of both the Africans and the Arabs. Christians, they believed—conveniently ignoring the Protestants and Catholics of the Confederate States of America who were fighting to keep their slaves in the 1860s—would never allow such a practice.

Khedive Ismail knew of the British opinion of slavery and hoped to curry their favor by sending Baker to eradicate the Nile slave trade. Whether the khedive personally opposed slavery is questionable, but he ordered Baker "to subdue to our authority the countries situated to the south of Gondokoro, to suppress the slave trade, to introduce a system of regular commerce, [and] to open to navigation the Great Lakes of the Equator."

In 1870, to carry out the khedive's plans, Baker started south from Khartoum. He reached Gondokoro in 1872 and managed to expel the great Arab trader in that area, Abu Sand. Next, Baker entered the area ruled by the Acholi. Unlike Mutesa, the Acholi had not welcomed the Arab traders, and they were pleased with the Englishman's work.

Baker's next step brought him into indirect conflict with Mutesa. Baker entered Bunyoro, Buganda's traditional rival. Under a new kabaka, Kabarega, Bunyoro had successfully regained some of the power it had held in the eighteenth century. Mutesa was worried about the growing strength of his kingdom's old enemy. Egyptian traders had helped Kabarega ascend to the throne of Bunyoro while the Zanzibari traders had joined with Mutesa in supporting Kabarega's rival and brother, Kabugurine. Mutesa kept up an active friendship with the Arab traders. In 1869, he sent the sultan of Zanzibar gifts of ivory and a baby elephant.

Baker's commission ended after four years. Although he claimed Bunyoro for the Egyptians, it was only a paper claim. Kabarega had refused to bow to the khedive, and Baker had thrown his support to Kabarega's new rival, Bionga. To Mutesa, all of this seemed very worrisome, indeed. The prospect of either a strong Bunyoro or a Bunyoro ruled by Egyptians posed grave threats to the independence of Buganda. Meanwhile, he continued to fear the growing influence of the Zanzibari traders in his kingdom. Just at this point, another Englishman appeared in Buganda.

Henry Morton Stanley arrived in Buganda in 1875. Stanley was an adventurer and a journalist who was under contract to newspapers in New York and London to report on life in the interior of Africa. Stanley was a devout Christian who engaged Mutesa in many conversations on the subject of religion. Mutesa agreed to welcome Christian missionaries to Buganda. His goal was to enlist new supporters who would help him ward off Egyptian invaders and help him control the growing influence of Islam.

Stanley wrote an open letter to a London newspaper asking for missionaries to serve in Buganda and explaining that the kabaka wanted

Christians to come and save his people. An anonymous philanthropist was so moved by the letter that he sent £5,000 to the Christian Missionary Society to aid in sending missionaries to Buganda. In the 1870s, Christians in England as well as Christians in Europe and the United States were absolutely convinced that the best thing for people in all parts of the world was to be brought into the Christian church. Non-Christians, including the followers of Mohammed, were considered to be heathens, damned to hell for eternity unless a missionary reached them before they died and converted them to Christianity.

No one believed in this Christian mission more fervently than the young men who accepted the funding of the Christian Missionary Society in 1876. Alexander MacKay, George Smith, and C. T. Wilson brought Christianity to Buganda. Their work was dangerous; Smith lived in Uganda only a year before being murdered. The new religion, however, would prove to be equally as dangerous to Uganda as to the missionaries.

The visit of adventurer-journalist Henry Morton Stanley to the court of Mutesa I paved the way for the admission of the Christian missionaries.

On top of each of three hills in Kampala is a large church—one is Protestant, one is Roman Catholic, and one is an Islamic mosque. Islam had come with the Arab traders. Shortly after the Protestant missionaries from England arrived in Buganda, a group of Roman Catholic missionaries from France, the White Fathers, established a mission in Buganda. The leader of this group, Father Landel, immediately tried to convince the kabaka that his missionaries represented the true Christian religion. The kabaka, already amazed by the violence of the religious arguments between Moslems and Christians, now learned that the arguments between different factions of the Christian religion, in this case Protestants and Roman Catholics, could be equally violent. Alexander MacKay, one of the original British missionaries who would last the longest in Buganda, reported telling the kabaka that he should not allow the Roman Catholics to stay in Buganda. MacKay noted, "I . . . distinctly told the King that we could not remain if [the White Fathers] were allowed to settle in the place." For his part, Father Landel was just as uncompromising and did his best to get Mutesa to renounce the Protestants and to embrace Roman Catholicism.

The missions founded by both groups became centers of learning for young men around the kabaka's court. Not only did the missionaries teach about religion, but they also instructed the Ganda boys in reading and writing. Even more intriguing, they were able to demonstrate machinery and other marvels of the industrial societies they had left behind. This was particularly true of MacKay, who had been an engineer before becoming a missionary. To the pre-industrial Ganda, MacKay combined mechanical wonders and religion, proof that the god he preached about was powerful indeed, perhaps even more powerful than the kabaka.

Mutesa I's reign lasted until his death in 1884. During the last five years of his life, he negotiated skillfully among the three warring religious groups in Buganda. Because his power as kabaka had been firmly entrenched before the establishment of the Christian missions, he was able to maintain his superiority over his people. He also maintained absolute control over the missions and from time to time expelled various groups from the court. In 1882, for example, Mutesa forced the White Fathers to move to the southern shore of Lake Victoria.

During the last years of Mutesa's reign, however, men at the court began to ally themselves with one or another of the new religions. Some clung tenaciously to the Islam of the Arab traders, who were quick to stir up rumors that the Protestants and Catholics were part of a European or Egyptian plot to take over the kingdom. Religion was becoming a political factor at the court of the kabaka. Different men, representing different religions, vied with each other for prominence at court. Only a strong kabaka could hold all these factions together and prevent civil war. Mutesa I was such a kabaka, but when he died, his successor, Mwanga, did not command the respect that his father did. Under Mwanga, the smoldering religious tensions would burst into full flame.

Mwanga was seventeen years old when his father died, and the lukiko voted him kabaka. His queen-sister, who had taken the English name of Rebecca, was a convert to Christianity, although Mwanga himself continued to practice lubareism. He had not been untouched, however, by the new religion. One of MacKay's goals was to end human sacrifice in Buganda. MacKay had had many conversations with Mutesa I about the indiscriminate way he tortured and killed his subjects. Mwanga had taken some of this to heart. At his coronation, he was the first kabaka not to have his brothers put to death. Nor did he order any ritual killings to celebrate his crowning. He also allowed the Roman Catholics to come back to the court. For the Christians, the ascension of Mwanga seemed to signal that Buganda was entering a modern, more civilized era.

Mwanga was not only young, but he was also described by MacKay as "fitful and fickle." In fairness to Mwanga, he was asked to administer, without much preparation, a kingdom that was quickly being drawn into the modern world. He did not have the time that his father had had to consolidate his own power before dealing with the competing factions that threatened to destroy his kingdom. By acceding to the Christian request that he no longer demonstrate his absolute power by wanton murder, Mwanga weakened himself in the eyes of his subjects. To condemn Mwanga for failing to hold the kingdom together is to ask too much of a young African king faced with a conflict that had brought down empires. Indeed, in Northern Ireland and in the Middle East today, religious conflicts continue to cause devastation and death and to defy the most sophisticated negotiators twentieth-century diplomacy can offer.

The first five years of Mwanga's reign, from 1884 through 1888, were filled with plots, counterplots, and bloodshed. Almost from the first, he lost control of the kingdom. The secret to the kabaka's success for generations had always been his ability to rise above clan affiliation. The religious factions provided as divisive an element as the clans once had. The chiefs, as always, were drawn from the most intelligent young men at the court. By the 1880s, the new generation of chiefs were literate—and they had usually been converted to one of the European religions. In addition, there was the third group, converts to Islam who were backed by the Arab traders. The Protestant missionaries, the White Fathers, and the Arab traders all stirred up trouble by helping their own supporters to advance at court.

Although Mwanga had not had anyone murdered when he assumed the throne, he soon decided that he needed to order some killings in order to assert his power. The Arab group convinced him early in 1885 that the missionaries—both Catholic and Protestant—were front men for a European plot to take over Buganda. In January 1885, Mwanga had three Christian converts put to death as a sign of his displeasure with the missionaries. Then in October, hearing that an Anglican bishop, James Hannington, was en route to Buganda, Mwanga had him murdered. The next May, the worst massacre of Mwanga's reign took place when he burned alive thirty young Christian converts who had refused to give up their new beliefs.

Throughout these troubled years, the Arab groups enjoyed a position of prominence at court. Mwanga, however, was as wary of them as he was of the Christians. There were rumors that the Zanzibari had plans to conquer all of East Africa; in 1887, a representative of Sultan Barghash of Zanzibar, Sulaiman bin Zcher, arrived at Mwanga's court and was instrumental in helping the Arab faction stir up Mwanga's hostility toward the Christians. Frustrated and confused, Mwanga attempted to expel the Arabs as well as the Christians from Buganda in 1888.

Mwanga's plot failed miserably. He became the first kabaka to be deposed. Because he had not put his brothers to death, there were numbers of them ready to take his place. The first was Kiwewa. He lasted only a short time because he refused to follow Islam. His younger brother, Kalema, took his place and ordered his subjects to follow Islam. Christian Gandas and those who still practiced lubareism fled or were driven from the kingdom.

Meanwhile, Mwanga had joined forces with the Christian missionaries who had also joined the exiles. After an unsuccessful expedition to recapture Buganda, Mwanga and the Christians were finally successful in 1889. Kalema joined with the old Buganda enemies in Bunyoro and retook the throne one more time, but he was unable to hold it, even with the help of Kabarega. By 1890, Mwanga sat securely on the throne of Buganda. He would not be deposed again by rival Ganda, but he would gradually lose power to a much larger force, the British Empire. The territory of Buganda and the surrounding kingdoms were about to become objects of attention in a fight that would consume the world for the next fifty years: the struggle for empire between the Germans and the British.

The religious warfare of the 1880s in Buganda had driven a wedge into that country that made it unstable and vulnerable to outside conquest. When Mwanga was restored as kabaka in 1890, it was with the agreement that all major political offices would be divided between Protestants and Roman Catholics. An Irish trader living in Uganda at the time noted how poorly this kind of division worked in his homeland.

As he wrote to the British commissioner of Uganda in 1894, "No doubt Buganda will be a thorn in Great Britain's side like my unfortunate country. . . ." For the time being, however, far from being a "thorn," Buganda seemed to the British to be a prize, one they must possess at all costs.

UGANDA AS A
BRITISH
PROTECTORATE

In the 1880s, German maps of the world began
to include the land that is modern Uganda in
the East African territory that they claimed for
the German Empire. By 1884, the Society for
German Colonization, a private organization,
had as one of its goals the inclusion of Uganda
in a worldwide German Empire.

The German organization posed a direct
threat to Britain's plans for East Africa. Although
the British exercised a great deal of influence
over northern and eastern Africa, they maintained a policy of free trade. They claimed that
they wanted the African kingdoms to remain
independent and free to trade with whatever

outsiders wished to trade with them. Great Britain did not want to spend the money necessary to occupy Uganda. At the same time, however, they did not want Germany to control the area.

The British and other European nations had developed a system that was halfway between allowing small nations to keep their independence and taking them over completely. Believing that nations like Buganda were incapable of negotiating and trading in a modern international market without the help of a white Christian industrialized nation, the nations of Europe divided areas of the nonindustrialized world into "spheres of influence." In July 1890, the British and the Germans arrived at a decision to partition territory in East Africa into spheres of influence for the two countries. The British received the territory that would become the twentieth-century nation of Uganda. All of this was accomplished with minimal conversations with Mwanga and almost no negotiation with the

A British cartoon of October 1911, shortly before World War I, depicted Germany as pretending to be shocked at Italy's imperialistic interest in Africa, while still carrying out its own exploitation of the continent.

other tribes and kingdoms that were incorporated into the territory.

To administer this area, the British government initially granted a charter to the British East Africa Company. This private organization was empowered by the king of England to govern the area between Kenya and Lake Victoria. Captain Frederick Lugard, on behalf of the British East Africa Company, met with Mwanga at the end of 1890 and explained to him the relationship between the company and Buganda. He promised the company's protection against Buganda's enemies. In return, Mwanga was to allow all Christian missionaries to teach in his country and to promise that he would make no trade agreements with other nations without the company's consent.

In the first years of official British domination in Buganda politics, continued warfare between the Roman Catholics, who enjoyed Mwanga's support, and the Protestants plagued the kingdom and the company. The internal strife proved to be more than a private company could handle; the British East Africa Company was on the verge of withdrawing. To lose control of this territory was unacceptable to the British government. The British Parliament stepped in and declared the Uganda Protectorate in 1894. Although this declaration applied solely to Buganda, plans for the extension of British power

*In 1890, Britain and Germany agreed to the
partition of East Africa into "spheres of influence."
The British received the territory that would
become twentieth-century Uganda.*

into other areas of Uganda were already in motion.

Because the British centered their administration of the Uganda Protectorate in Buganda, their opinion of the other tribes and kingdoms in East Africa was heavily colored by the Ganda's relationship with each tribe. For example, the British helped the Ganda invade Bunyoro and granted some of Bunyoro's territory to Buganda. By the beginning of the twentieth century, the British had successfully extended their control over Bunyoro, Toro, and Ankole. These Bantu kingdoms had some knowledge of the British from missionaries and traders. Like the Ganda, they had willingly enlisted the aid of one foreign group or another in their attempts to increase the size of their own kingdoms. Because they were Bantu, their tribal organization was similar to that of the Bantu. But none of these other kingdoms had the efficient central government of the kabaka of Buganda. Nevertheless, all of the leaders of these areas had armies and carried on sophisticated negotiations with Arab traders, with the British, and with Sudanese and Egyptians during their wars of conquest. To them, the establishment of British control over their lives did not come as a complete shock. Although they neither agreed to this nor wanted it, they all, especially Bunyoro, viewed the coming of the British as evidence that Buganda had again won in the old tribal struggle.

For other tribes that would be absorbed into the area of the Uganda Protectorate, however, the coming of the British was a rude shock that eventually ended their way of life. The pastoral, nomadic, and warrior tribes of the northern and northeastern area of the protectorate had never agreed to British rule; in fact, many of them had never even seen an Englishman. Among these were the Turkana, the Langi, the Sebei, the Teso, the Bugisu, the Bukedi, the Acholi, and the Karamojong. The imposition of British rule on these peoples, with the collaboration of the Ganda, created deep hostility toward Buganda, hostility that would flare into civil war in the twentieth century.

The Karamojong are perhaps the best example of an indigenous group in Uganda who cling proudly to their old way of life. The Karamojong are a Hamitic, cattle people. The men are very tall and until recently wore nothing but leather sandals. Their hair is dressed with mud and decorated with colorful ostrich feathers. A section of the male Karamojong's lip is cut for the insertion of a white shell that is never removed. The Karamojong women wear cowhide skirts and hoops of beaded wire necklaces that are never removed.

The district of Karamoja is semiarid, and to graze the cattle that count as wealth to the Karamojong, the tribe moves constantly within their province. This tribe, like so many other smaller

The Karamojong live in an extremely dry area.
They are easily recognized by their distinctive hair style
and the white shell inserted through a cut in the lip.

nomadic tribes, did not agree to British control and for the most part resisted British attempts to change their way of life. Since the land they occupied was not especially valuable, the British, though nominally ruling the Karamojong, were content to let them continue their old ways.

To most British colonial administrators, the Karamojong symbolized "heathen Africans," incapable of dealing with the British or learning the lessons of a modern industrialized society. At best, the Karamojong appeared as handsome, exotic creatures whose tribal dances and ceremonies were wonderful occasions for intrepid tourists and whose stern, decorated faces made great photographs for the *National Geographic*. Sadly for the Karamojong and other traditional tribes, the protectorate would bring major changes in their lives, no matter how they resisted.

Modern medicine, although primitive by European standards, brought a longer life expectancy and more people to sustain on marginal land. Big-game hunters depleted the wild animals that the Karamojong stalked. And, finally, scientific attacks on the tsetse fly changed the number of cattle that the Karamojong had maintained for generations. All of this was done, of course, by well-intentioned British colonists who truly believed that the Karamojong—like people all over the world—could live best under British standards of justice, wealth, hygiene, and religion.

The agreement signed by Mwanga in 1894 had taken away much of the kabaka's control and had attempted to divide power among the three religious/political factions—the Protestants, the Moslems, and the Roman Catholics—that had divided Buganda throughout the 1890s. Since the United Kingdom was officially a Protestant nation, a Protestant, Apolo Kagwa, held the important post of prime minister, or katikiro.

In 1895, George Wilson was appointed by Great Britain to regulate the government of Buganda. He increased the importance of the parliament, or lukiko, which was headed by Kagwa, a shrewd, intelligent politican who viewed the British system favorably because it allowed for the katikiro to share the power that had once belonged to the kabaka alone. In short, Wilson proposed to make Buganda a constitutional monarchy not unlike Great Britain.

Mwanga became increasingly unhappy with this new form of government, and in 1897 he rebelled against the British authorities. For nearly three years, he carried out a minor guerrilla war in a futile attempt to rid his kingdom of the British. To Mwanga's chagrin, few of his citizens joined him. They had learned that the British were stronger; besides, some, including Kagwa, were enjoying their positions in the new government. In 1900, Mwanga was finally defeated; the British had named his infant son, Daudi Chwa, kabaka in 1897. Kagwa and two other chiefs served as his regents until he grew old enough to reign by himself.

During this rebellion, Mwanga had fled to Ankole. The British took this opportunity to add Ankole officially to the protectorate that now had active British administrators in Busoga, Bunyoro, and Toro.

To formalize the changes in the relationship between the kabaka and the lukiko, the British and Kagwa signed the Agreement of 1900, legislation that set the course of Uganda's development in the twentieth century. Buganda was firmly established as one province within the larger British Protectorate. Although the kabaka was to remain as king and to be accorded the title of "His Highness," he no longer had complete control over his government. He shared power with the katikiro and with a chief justice and treasurer, new offices created by the agreement. The lukiko would serve as the legislative branch of the government.

Taxation and land ownership were other features of the agreement. The British were to be paid a hut tax by every male Ganda, although the taxes would be collected by Ganda tax collectors. The British imposed their ideas of land ownership on the Ganda. Land was parceled out to individual landowners, a new concept in Buganda, and one that would increase the wealth and thus the importance of the major chiefs who received the greatest amounts of land.

The agreement in Buganda was similar to agreements made with Toro in 1900 and Ankole in 1901. Although no formal agreement was made with Bunyoro until the 1930s, in practice much of the same kind of government structure was developed there in 1900. By 1900, the British had established constitutional monarchies in the four traditional kingdoms within the Uganda Protectorate.

In 1919, the British Parliament passed the Native Law Ordinance. This legislation extended the type of government existing in the kingdoms to the outlying tribal areas. The British governor of the Uganda Protectorate, according to law, had the right to recognize or develop any legislative body he chose to administer the law in the various districts that lay outside the area of the four kingdoms.

In the Kigezi District a legislative body was organized in 1927 and in Lango in 1935. The reason for the delay was the resistance of the tribes in these areas, like the Karamojong, to giving up their traditional management of tribal affairs and replacing them with the British system. The British viewed resistance on the part of these tribes as further evidence that they were a backward people unready for civilization.

Despite the numerous traders, missionaries, and British government officials who had made the trek to Lake Victoria since the 1840s, at the end of the nineteenth century there was still only one reliable way to get there—walk. Any equipment that was introduced to Buganda had to be carried into the kingdom. Human porters were the major form of transportation throughout East Africa.

With the growth of British colonial government in Uganda came a corresponding increase in the cost of administering the protectorate. The hut tax that had been levied in 1900 was not enough to pay for officials' salaries and the improvements that the British wished to make. Furthermore, outside the four kingdoms, the hut tax was difficult to collect. Native Ugandans had long used cowrie shells to pay for goods and services; in 1901, the British refused to allow cowrie shells to be used as money. This severely limited the average tribesman's ability to pay his taxes. Finally, the law allowed for the Ugandans to pay their taxes in produce. An entire village might join together to capture an elephant or hippopotamus to pay taxes. One hippo paid the tax for one hundred huts, an elephant for one thousand huts, but the hippo or the elephant was of limited use to the British government. The Parliament in Great Britain was reluctant to lose money in Uganda. They believed a colony should have some source of money that would enable it to pay for itself.

Because of the fertile soil in Uganda, the British decided to develop a cash crop that could be exported from Uganda at a profit. The development of such a crop depended on building a modern transportation system. The profits from the crop would have to be substantial enough to pay for the construction of the new transportation system.

In 1899–1900, the cost of running the Uganda Protectorate was £296,226, most of which was paid by the British government. In 1914–15, the last year that Uganda cost the British anything, the price of its management was only £10,000. The rest of the £289,213 needed to run the protectorate in that year was raised by taxes. One crop had changed the economic picture in Uganda. That crop was cotton.

Cotton production grew rapidly in Uganda. In the first place, the soil and growing conditions were ideal. In the second place, the governor of the protectorate placed strict controls on the type of cotton to be grown, the ways in which it was to be ginned, and the amount of acreage to be planted.

The British in Uganda had founded a cash crop on which to base a modern economy, but they faced the question of how to transport the crop. By the end of the 1890s, the Uganda Railway had been built from Mombasa, a port city in the British colony of Kenya, to the eastern shore of Lake Victoria. Water transportation from Kampala across Lake Victoria to the railroad was the easier part of the problem to solve. The bigger issue was how to get the cotton to Kampala.

The governor of the protectorate, Hesketh

Bell, began the development of an ambitious transportation system to solve the problem of getting the cotton to market. By 1907, cotton was the protectorate's most valuable export, and by 1910 cotton moved to market on a well-built system of modern roads. By 1912, a railroad had been constructed from Jinja to Kakindu in the heart of the rich eastern cotton-growing area. At the same time, travel off the main roads or railway routes remained extremely difficult. For example, although a road had been constructed from Kampala to Toro in 1912, it contained a 14-mile (23-km) gap where the territory was too rugged for road building. All goods traveling along that gap had to be carried by human porters, usually on men's heads.

Because of the rapid development of the cotton industry, the city of Kampala by 1914—the year of the outbreak of World War I—was a bustling economic center with roads, railway stations, banks, and government offices. Because the British had instituted private ownership of land, the chiefs in Buganda who owned the largest cotton farms prospered personally, even as the nation grew wealthier. With their new prosperity came new political and social prominence. Accustomed as they had been to the Ganda hierarchical structure, the chiefs and the peasant workers adjusted easily to a new economic system that mirrored the old tribal social order.

For Uganda at this time, rapid economic change was achieved peacefully. That some people grew wealthier than others did not seem at all strange to the Baganda. For generations, they had lived in a society with rigid ranks where chiefs lived more lavishly than peasants, and the kabaka lived most lavishly of all. What was especially remarkable about the growth of large-scale agriculture in Uganda is that, for the most part, the land was owned by native Ugandans. In other areas of the British Empire, the pattern of agricultural development had been much different. In general, white Englishmen and Europeans owned large plantations that were cultivated by native populations. In Uganda, however, the natives were both owners and cultivators. In the 1920s, the production of coffee was added to the country's export economy. By 1945—the end of World War II—coffee outstripped cotton as a major revenue producer for Uganda.

Until 1945, the basic patterns of life in the Uganda Protectorate remained much the same. In administering the protectorate, the British had hoped to develop a self-sufficient economy that would pay the costs of supervision and would introduce a modern market economy to the interior of Africa. By the end of World War I, they had achieved both goals, and for the period between the two world wars, the British introduced little that was new to Uganda. Cotton and coffee continued to produce strong revenues, even during the Great Depression, and by material measures—increases in automobiles, miles of railroad track, numbers of houses with tin roofs and windows, sales of bicycles—life for ordinary Ugandans became more modernized.

What the British failed to do during this period of time was to allow Ugandans to become fully involved in running their country's economy. Although Ugandans grew the major crops, the processing, marketing, and banking industries were controlled by the British or by a significant Asian population that had immigrated from other parts of the British Empire to Uganda. Once there, they filled the ranks of the merchant class, running shops and banks and holding intermediate civil service positions. In this way, Ugandans were kept from developing an effective middle class that could sustain the economy when the British left.

The British justification for allowing the Ugandans only limited participation in the economic development of the country was based on the misguided judgment that the native peoples of the African interior were backward, uncivilized people who could not handle the complexities of directing a modern, capitalist nation.

The British who felt this way pointed out that fewer than one hundred years had passed since John Speke "discovered" the kingdom of Mutesa I. Torture and cannibalism had been common practices in his kingdom, and in spite of the relative social and political development among the Bantu, little in the way of a barter economy existed.

The people of interior Africa are as naturally intelligent and talented as people anywhere. However, the geographic factors that kept Europeans from the interior of "darkest Africa" for so long had also hindered the development of a trade network among the people living there. Unlike the people of North America or Asia or Europe, the people of Africa suffered real geographic isolation. The lack of internal rivers made communication extremely difficult. The exchange of products and ideas with coastal towns that so stimulated rapid growth on other continents was missing in Africa. In addition to the lack of waterways, the diseases that dominated the interior made it impossible to depend on beasts of burden for transportation.

In the face of little or no communication and transportation, the remarkable thing about the Ugandans, particularly in Buganda, was the sophistication of their political and social organization by the mid-nineteenth century. With virtually no exchange of ideas outside their immediate area, the Ganda had designed a government and society so familiar to the British that their colonization of the area was relatively peaceful and the colonial administrators dealt amiably and, for the most part, equally with chiefs whom they recognized as their counterparts.

In the years between the end of World War II in 1945 and the emergence of Uganda as an independent nation in 1962, two British errors would create more and more tension in the country: their reliance on the Baganda as representatives of all Ugandans and their failure to incorporate any Ugandans into the middle management of the nation's economy.

UGANDA RETURNS
TO INDEPENDENCE

Between 1939 and 1945, Great Britain was embroiled in World War II. England and the Allies fought to free Europe from German domination and to liberate the countries that had been taken over by Hitler against their will. The citizens of the various countries in the British Empire, including Uganda, were drawn into the conflict on behalf of the Allies.

The end of the war in 1945 brought Allied victory over Germany. For six years, the Americans, British, French, and their allies had proclaimed that all people in the world should be free to choose their own form of government. This "self-determination of peoples" had also been the professed goal of World War I. When that war had ended, however, the British, among others, had not given up their colonial possessions, and the promise of the war had never been fulfilled. Disillusionment with the failed ideals of World War I had been partially responsible for World War II.

This time, the victors were determined to do a better job of living up to the ideals for which they had fought. At the end of the war, England's King George VI announced to Parliament, "In the territories for which my government is responsible, they will work actively to promote the welfare of my peoples, to develop the economic life of the territories and to give my peoples all practical guidance in their march to self-government."

Perhaps even more important than the British resolve to cooperate in helping their colonies achieve independence was the determination of native citizens throughout the British Empire to take back control of their countries. Certainly this was true in Uganda and throughout Africa. As the war drew to a close, a new group of young Ugandans began to protest British control of their government. Within a few short years, their protests would lead to independence for the nation, but a nation plagued by the tensions of the pre-colonial and colonial period.

As had been the case for other movements during Uganda's modern history, the movement toward independence was centered in Buganda. During the last year of the war, a number of riots occurred in Buganda. The protesters tended to be young Africans who were frustrated by their lack of power in their country. Not only were they angry at the idea that Uganda was controlled by foreigners, but they were also upset by the apparent collaboration between certain wealthy chiefs and the British rulers. Over the years, the membership of the lukiko had become rigid. Rather than being a democratic legislature, chosen by the people of Buganda, the lukiko was composed of major landowning chiefs. The young Africans believed that these chiefs did not want to change the balance of political power in Uganda as long as they enjoyed Great Britain's favor.

The national legislature established by the British in 1921 drew representatives from the four kingdoms and from the other provinces but did not provide an answer to the young Africans' desire for political office. Because of the old tribal animosities, Africans had been uninterested in sitting in a legislature that would ask them to share power with other tribes. As a result, the national legislative council was disproportionately full of white Englishmen representing their provincial interests. The Ganda and the other African peoples preferred to handle local matters through tribal legislatures like the lukiko. These tended to be nondemocratic councils of older chiefs. In the postwar atmosphere of freedom and independence, the new generation of Africans could not see an opportunity for real political participation on either a national or a tribal level.

During 1945, the treasurer, or *omuwanika*, of Uganda, Serwano Kulubya, was under attack by the protesters. Wartime had brought rising prices and inflation, and the omuwanika was the logical target for economic protest. When he resigned, the British, in conjunction with a new katikiro, Martin Luther Nsibirwa, attempted to rid the lukiko of any chiefs who would not give total support to the protectorate. At British urging, the new members of the lukiko agreed to give the kabaka greater powers. This further movement away from democracy led to more protests and to the assassination of Nsibirwa.

The new katikiro, Mikaeri Kawalya-Kagwa, joined with the protectorate to make further changes in the lukiko. The division between the people of Buganda and the council of chiefs grew wider. In a modern age, the chiefs no longer could command the loyalty of their clans as they once had. They were increasingly viewed as a privileged upper class who were pawns in the hands of the British. The British, by continuing their policy of governing through traditional native authorities, made two big mistakes. First, they retarded the development of democracy in Buganda because the traditional Ganda society was far from democratic. Second, by ignoring the Ganda's reluctance to participate in a national legislature, they aided in the disunity of Uganda as a whole.

During the immediate postwar years, the situation in Uganda remained much the same. The British widened the membership and responsibilities of the national legislative council so that by 1950 its fourteen official members and fourteen nonofficial members were drawn from Africans, Asians, and Europeans, with Africans holding half the seats and the other two groups sharing the other half. African representation was drawn proportionally from all over Uganda. The northern, western, and eastern provincial councils as well as the Buganda lukiko were entitled to nominate councillors.

The Buganda lukiko never cooperated fully with the legislative council because they viewed it as a threat to their lawmaking power. Neverthelss, the British continued to view the council as an important step in preparing the protectorate for self-government.

There were other aspects of the British plan for an independent Uganda that did not meet with Baganda favor. Under the British scheme, Uganda would become a democratic federation. Buganda, the other kingdoms, and the provinces would maintain a federal relationship to a central government. Each would continue to exercise a great deal of control over local affairs. The proposed form of government would be similar in its shared powers to that of the national and state governments in the United States.

Buganda—at least the kabaka and members of the lukiko—never agreed to this plan. The kabaka reminded the British of the agreement between Great Britain and Uganda in 1900. He asserted that Buganda and Great Britain had signed a treaty as two independent nations and that a federal system would violate that treaty.

The kabaka at this time was an urbane, sophisticated young man who had been educated in Great Britain. Officially *Mutesa II*, he was known as King Freddy by his supporters and by the international jet set crowd with whom he socialized. His experience, outlook, and style of leadership were a far cry from those of his great-grandfather, Mutesa I. However, he shared Mutesa's loyalty to Buganda and hostility toward surrounding tribes.

In 1953, Mutesa II asked the British to grant Buganda separate independent status. He also asked that Gandan affairs be transferred from the colonial office in London to the Foreign Office as a sign that Buganda had equal status with Great Britain as a nation. As a result of these demands, which contradicted the wishes of the British government, Mutesa II was deported in November 1953.

The governor of the protectorate in 1954 presented the lukiko with a choice. If the lukiko would accept national federation and curtail the

Mutesa II ("King Freddy") at the Parliament building of Buganda, in a reception marking Uganda's independence. To his right and left, representing the British government, are the Duke and Duchess of Kent.

kabaka's powers so that the kabaka and the lu-kiko constituted a real constitutional monarchy, then the lukiko could either invite Mutesa II to return or elect a new kabaka. Buganda rejoiced when Mutesa II returned to his throne in the fall of 1955.

For the next seven years, the British and Buganda hammered out the details of an independent federation. The crisis in Buganda had been averted and had also diverted the attention of the rest of the country from other serious problems that would plague the new nation.

In October 1962, bonfires were lit throughout Uganda. Speaking to crowds outside the kabaka's palace on Mengo Hill, Mutesa II announced, "Uganda is determined that she will never again become an extension of Europe." After years of preparation for self-government, the four traditional kingdoms and the major tribes of the outlying provinces of Uganda had agreed on a government.

Uganda became the fifth African nation to gain independence in 1962. The continent that had once been divided among the various European empires was at long last dividing into individual states—over thirty of them by the time Uganda joined their ranks as an independent nation. The new nation had enjoyed considerable prosperity since World War II. Coffee accounted for half the nation's export income, and coffee and cotton profits ensured that the

In 1962, school children wave flags—six stripes of black, gold, and red—in celebration of Uganda's independence after over seventy years of British rule.

nation enjoyed a favorable balance of trade. Although the per capita income of $65 seemed low by Western industrial standards, the figure was substantial for Africa. Most of Uganda, because of its fertile land, did not face the problems of drought and starvation that challenged so many of the emerging African nations.

At the time of independence, there were nearly seven million Ugandans, among whom eleven thousand were white and seventy thousand were Asian. The small percentage of non-African citizens set Uganda apart from its East African neighbors, Kenya, Tanganyika, and Zanzibar. In those nations, the greatest issue for independence was establishing the balance of power between the descendants of the white colonists and the indigenous African people. In Uganda, however, the problems would continue to revolve around economic, regional, and tribal conflicts.

The new government was designed around a complex balance of power between Buganda and the rest of the country. Buganda retained a large measure of autonomy by having an elected lukiko that controlled internal affairs. Meanwhile, an elected national legislature, with its headquarters at Kampala, made laws for the nation as a whole. There were three political parties represented in the national legislature: the Kabaka Yekka, the Democratic Party (DP), and the Uganda People's Congress (UPC). The Kabaka Yekka was the royalist party backing Mutesa II and drew its greatest support from the Baganda. The DP represented the new country's Roman Catholic faction. Finally, the UPC was composed of northerners under the leadership of Milton Obote. Faced with choosing between the DP and the UPC, King Freddy formed a coalition government with Obote's party.

In the new government, Obote was prime minister and Mutesa II was head of state. This uneasy partnership was not destined to last long. By 1964, Obote controlled a majority of the seats in the legislature. More important for Uganda's future, he had come to rely on the military to maintain his control. The army had become a wing of the prime minister's party. The seeds for military dictorship had been sown.

Apollo Milton Obote, the man who successfully challenged "King Freddy" for control of the new government, was the son of peasant farmers and a member of the Langi tribe, one of the northern Sudanic peoples. As a young man, Obote had studied politics in Kenya under Jomo Kenyatta and Tom Mboya. Initially he believed in the unity of all of East Africa.

Apollo Milton Obote was a disciple of Jomo Kenyatta, the leader of neighboring Kenya. Obote was able to rally support of northern tribes to overthrow King Freddy's government.

The army that supported Obote was drawn from the northern tribes. Throughout the years of their rule, the British had enlisted men from the Acholi, the Langi, and other northern tribes for the Uganda Rifles and the police force. The northern tribesmen with their warrior heritage, living on land that did not sustain agriculture as well as the land in the south, saw in the army a chance for employment and power.

Chief among Obote's military supporters was a strong, enthusiastic, young man from the Kakwa tribe who had risen through the ranks of the colonial army. Prior to Uganda's independence, Sergeant Major Idi Amin held the highest rank an African could hold. He provided the force that kept Obote in power. Obote rewarded him by giving him greater and greater control of the armed forces.

In February 1966, several members of the legislature publicly questioned some of Amin's activities, alleging that he was involved in gold smuggling in Zaire. Among the accusers were three members of Obote's cabinet. Within a few weeks, Obote arrested these officials, suspended the legislature, threw out the constitution, dismissed Mutesa II as head of state, and appointed Amin commander of the army. Democracy ended in Uganda. Civil war began.

On April 15, 1966, Obote declared a new constitution. Under its provisions, he was the executive president of Uganda. The kabaka of Buganda—as well as the kings of Busoga, Bunyoro, and Toro—were barred from holding political office. The Baganda did not submit easily. The lukiko refused to recognize Obote's government within Buganda and ordered him to leave their territory.

In May, Amin's troops crushed the Baganda resistance, stormed the palace, and forced King Freddy into exile. The cool, urbane Freddy hailed a taxi outside the palace that took him to the edge of the city. From there, he walked for four weeks through the countryside, eventually reaching a safe haven in Zaire. From Zaire, he flew to London, where he lived in exile until his death in 1969. His kingdom was divided into four military districts by Obote, who declared that he was "freeing the common man from royalty." When Mutesa II heard of this decision, he said, "I think it can be done on paper, but never in the hearts of my people."

One of the dangers of an authoritarian government is that it does not allow for the legitimate, peaceful expression of ideas that oppose those of the dictator. It is almost impossible for a new leader to emerge without bloodshed. Milton Obote created a monster when he allowed Idi Amin to build the Uganda army under his control. In a very short time, Amin rivaled Obote for control of the government.

Idi Amin Dada (Dada was his family name) had been born in the small village of Arua, located in the West Nile region. His parents were

*Idi Amin seized power in 1971 in a coup
that marked the beginning of one of the
bloodiest chapters in Uganda's history.*

subsistence farmers, and in order to have a higher standard of living, Amin, like many young men of the northern districts, enlisted in the king's Uganda Rifles. He quickly rose from cook to noncommissioned officer. Amin was a strong, loyal, and courageous member of the colonial army. He fought for the British in Kenya during the Mau Mau rebellion and was rewarded for his valor with another promotion. At the time of independence, the British chose Amin as one of the Africans to be commissioned as second lieutenant in the new Ugandan army. Amin got along well with the rank and file of the army. He was suspicious of men with university educations and was a devout practitioner of Islam. Following the law of the Koran, he had four wives by the time he was associated with Obote.

Amin's willingness to play second fiddle to Milton Obote was short-lived. Under his leadership, the army had grown nine times since 1962, and the majority of the new recruits came from tribes related to Amin's own Kakwa tribe. The Acholi and the Langi, who tended to support their kinsman, Obote, received fewer and fewer promotions. Rumors grew that Amin was rounding up Acholi and Langi and executing them.

Near the end of 1969, an assassination attempt was made on Obote. Amin disappeared for several hours, heightening suspicion that he had masterminded the failed coup. Then, in 1970, Obote deprived Amin of operational control of the army. By giving him a ceremonial role in the government, Obote hoped to thwart his former lieutenant's growing power. His plan failed. In January 1971, while Milton Obote attended a conference in Singapore, he learned of yet another Amin-directed assassination plot and ordered Amin's arrest. But Amin had more power than Obote. By the end of January 1971, Amin controlled the government in Kampala.

From 1971 until 1979, Idi Amin ruled Uganda. His leadership was marked by ruthless execution of his enemies, destruction of the nation's economy, militant posturing and buffoonery in international affairs, and, finally, open warfare with Tanzania.

Estimates of the number of people killed during Amin's regime range from two hundred thousand to half a million. Whatever the accurate figure, the fact is that Idi Amin's army carried out mass murders of many thousands who opposed Amin. Frequently, mass executions were based on tribal affiliation. The rumors of Acholi and Langi murders were no longer rumors. By 1971, Amin ordered the murder of thousands of soldiers whose only crime was their membership in either of these two tribes.

Idi Amin will long be remembered as the leader of a regime noted for its ruthlessness and cruelty.

Nor were the military the only victims of Amin's terrorism. A police organization, the Public Safey Unit, and an intelligence organization, the State Research Bureau, sought out and eliminated, by torture and murder, alleged civilian enemies of Amin. One of the favorite methods of execution was to crush the victim's head with a sledgehammer.

When Amin was overthrown in 1979, the liberating troops found a torture chamber in the basement of the presidential mansion. This was the headquarters of the State Research Bureau. A gully in the floor was apparently used to sluice the victims' blood out of the basement. By the end of his rule, Amin had ordered the murders of Uganda's chief justice, the vice-chancellor of the university, the Anglican archbishop, the army chief of staff, eleven members of the cabinet, and the mayor of Kampala. These men were only the most famous of Amin's hundreds of thousands of victims.

Although the murder of human beings was the most shocking aspect of Amin's regime, the destruction of the economy was also devastating. First, Amin destroyed the nation's budget because of the size of the military force that he maintained. A nation the size of Uganda simply could not afford such a large standing army. Second, to build the loyalty of the army, Amin purchased all kinds of presents for his favorite officers, including expensive cars and homes.

The army was allowed to poach at will in the Ruwenzori National Park, one of the world's finest game preserves. Estimates of the number of elephants killed run as high as 90 percent of the park's population. Equally as destructive to the Ugandan economy was Amin's abrupt decision in 1972 to expel all Asians from Uganda.

Throughout the course of the twentieth century, a small but vital and generally prosperous Asian population—predominantly Indians and Pakistani—had staffed Uganda's stores, banks, law offices, engineering firms, and hospitals. Generally well educated and wealthy, the Asians had never enjoyed nor sought political power. They had been victims of subtle social and political discrimination from both Europeans and Africans, but they had quietly carved a niche for themselves and were disproportionately represented in Uganda's professional middle class.

In August 1972, Amin ordered the seventy thousand Asians living in Uganda to leave the country within three months. Furthermore, they had to leave all their financial assets behind. Each Asian was permitted to carry only $140 out of the country. Approximately half of the Asians living in Uganda had retained British passports they had been issued during the days of the protectorate. Many thousands of others were Ugandan citizens. In the face of international outrage at this action, Amin said, "God was directing me . . . [the Asians] were retarding the

economy of the country. We are not racist. The decision was purely in the interests of [Uganda]."

The departure of the Asians left Uganda with a serious shortage of lawyers, engineers, doctors, and businessmen, which led to further deterioration of the economy. The road system fell into such disrepair that the following joke went around Kampala: "If you see a man driving a straight line in Uganda, you know he's drunk." The failure to maintain highways and road lines hampered Uganda's ability to get exports to market. The loss of Asian civil engineers and middlemen in the cotton and coffee industries added to the economic hardship. Without the *dukawallahs*, as the Asian shopkeepers were known, commercial life in Kampala ground to a halt.

For a time during the mid-1970s, the soaring price of coffee on the international market provided the Ugandan government with enough revenue to keep the economy afloat in spite of Amin's excesses. However, by 1978, the economy was in disarray. Inflation was rampant. The average worker made about $1.50 a day, less

East Asians—ordered by Idi Amin to leave Uganda— are shown here arriving in England, the first of many thousands to emigrate.

than the price of a bottle of beer or a pint of milk. Sugar cost $3 a pound, gasoline cost $50 to $65 per gallon, and soap was $3 a bar. Even at these prices, some of these commodities were hard to find.

Finally, Amin's actions led to economic boycott by nations that had once been vital to Uganda's balance of trade. In October 1978, U.S. President Jimmy Carter initiated a trade embargo that stopped American purchase of Ugandan coffee. By this point, coffee accounted for 90 percent of Uganda's income, and the United States was a major customer, responsible for one-third of the total amount. Great Britain, Israel, and the United States, all of whom had once provided aid and markets to Uganda, eventually cut off their support. Amin was left with few allies, chief among them Colonel Muammur Qaddafy of Libya, a fellow Moslem, but a man whose country faced too many financial difficulties of its own to be able to do much for Uganda.

Amin professed to be a devout Moslem. He expressed his beliefs through violent hostility toward both Christians and Jews. His antipathy to the Acholi and the Langi troops stemmed not only from their tribal affiliation but also from the fact that they were Christian. Through intimidation and murder, he hoped to purge the army of non-Moslems.

In spite of his animosity toward Christians, Amin's greatest hatred was reserved for Jews.

He counted Qaddafy as his staunchest ally. To demonstrate his friendship with the Libyan dictator, he expelled all Israelis from Uganda in 1972. Amin publicly praised Adolf Hitler for his murder of European Jews during World War II and boasted that he would erect a statue in honor of Der Führer, as Hitler was known. When Arab terrorists murdered Jewish athletes at the Munich Olympics, Amin praised their actions. He allowed the Palestinians to build terrorist training camps in Uganda.

Amin's support of terrorism earned him little respect from the world community, and in 1976 he was highly embarrassed by the Israelis. An Air France flight, en route to Paris from Tel Aviv, was hijacked by Palestinian terrorists. The hijackers refueled the plane in Libya and then landed at Entebbe airfield, where Idi Amin, dressed in a cowboy hat, went out to the hangar where the passengers were being held hostage, to welcome them to Uganda.

For several days, Amin gave the hijackers shelter while they negotiated with the Israeli government. Then, after several days of stalled talks, a group of Israeli commandos swooped down on Entebbe and liberated all but one of the hostages. The exception was an elderly American woman who had been hospitalized in Uganda. Enraged and humiliated, Amin ordered her murder and the execution of four radar operators at Entebbe who had failed to warn of the Israelis' approach.

Amin's Arab supporters urged a United Nations resolution condemning Israel's action. The resolution failed. The British broke off diplomatic relations with Uganda, the first time they had ever done so to a Commonwealth nation. Kenya cut off petroleum exports to Amin and demanded payment of the $54 million trade debt owed them by Uganda.

Kenya's action was especially significant. At the beginning of Amin's reign, other African leaders, although not completely approving of his methods, withheld public criticism of "Big Daddy," as he was referred to in the Western press. Many African nations were struggling to be taken seriously as independent countries. Amin was strong and colorful and commanded international attention. His fellow African heads of state were reluctant to criticize him.

The Organization of African Unity (OAU) is committed to nonintervention in the internal affairs of member countries, but by the late 1970s, many of the members of the OAU made an exception in the case of Uganda. Far from representing African leaders as strong and capable, Amin now appeared to show the world that Africans were uncivilized and barbaric. The thirteen African members of the Commonwealth of Nations agreed with that group's 1977 resolution condemning Idi Amin for "sustained disregard for human life and massive violation of basic human rights."

No African leader was more outspoken in his opposition to Amin than President Julius Nyerere of Tanzania. Nyerere hated Amin for presenting a terrible and ludicrous image of Africans to the world. For example, Amin appeared before the OAU dressed in a cowboy hat and carrying pearl-handled revolvers. Nyerere also blamed Amin for the destruction of the East African economy. In theory, the two nations were allies and economic partners with Kenya in the British East Africa community. As early as 1971, the first year of Amin's reign, there were border skirmishes between Tanzanian and Ugandan troops. As a Nairobi newspaper sadly reported, this was the first time since independence that East African neighbors had slain each other.

Relations between Tanzania and Uganda remained tense throughout the 1970s. Milton Obote had sought refuge in Tanzania when he was overthrown by Amin, and Amin accused Nyerere of arming Obote's guerrilla supporters. In October 1978, Amin launched an invasion against Tanzania. Many observers believed that he did this to divert attention from the problems at home. Serious fighting within the Simba (Lion) and Chui (Leopard) battalions of the army weakened Amin's control of the military. He hoped to regain this support by providing Ugandans with a common external enemy.

Amin's plan backfired. Calling Amin "a murderer, a liar and a savage," Nyerere ordered

Tanzanian troops to fight back and to invade Uganda. By March, the Tanzanians were 70 miles (113 km) from Kampala and gaining ground. Amin made a radio address to the nation in which he asked, "Ugandans who believe in god . . . [to] pray day and night." In spite of military aid from Libya, Amin could not hold on. On April 23, 1979, he, his wives, and nearly forty children fled to Saudi Arabia. Ugandans prayed that the bloodiest chapter in their history had ended.

UGANDA IN
THE 1980s

With the exile of Idi Amin, Ugandans hoped that their nation could return to peace and prosperity. Milton Obote had waited out Amin's regime in Tanzania. He hoped to return to power. However, many Ugandans had not forgotten that Obote had instituted the military dictatorship that gave rise to Amin. Nor had they forgotten Obote's early ties to Amin and his drift toward socialism in the late 1960s.

In 1979, a group of Ugandans in exile, representing over twenty political factions, met in Moshi, Tanzania, to choose a temporary leader until elections could be held. The man they chose was a Ganda, the sixty-seven-year-old former vice-chancellor of Makerere University, Yusuf Lule. Lule's task was to head the eleven-man Uganda National Liberation Front that would serve as an interim ruling body.

The nation that Lule headed was a devastated one. Coffee prices worldwide had dropped significantly from $8,000 a ton in 1977 to $2,000 a ton in 1979, severely hurting the country's economic base. In an act of amnesty, twenty thousand prisoners were released from Ugandan jails. Some of these were legitimately behind bars for murder, robbery, and other serious crimes. They immediately took up their old trades, terrorizing people in cities. During Amin's years in office, cotton production had declined by 80 percent, copper by 50 percent, and tourism by 100 percent. The inflation rate had jumped 800 percent. The northern areas of the country were suffering drought and famine.

The problems facing Uganda were too much for Lule's leadership. He lasted in office less than three months. He was succeeded by Godfrey Binaisa, an Obote supporter. Binaisa was an attorney who had been trained in British univer-

Karamojong supporters welcome Milton Obote back from exile. In elections generally believed to be corrupt, Obote was returned to power.

sities and who had served as a general under Obote. Binaisa lasted one year. Then, in elections held in 1980 and generally believed to be unfair and corrupt, Milton Obote was returned to power.

Although Obote promised economic recovery and democracy, his second term in office brought Uganda further economic hardship and another harsh military dictatorship. Obote had won the election through fraud. For example, his supporters, who included much of the military, controlled the media in Uganda. Radio stations refused to carry any campaign speeches except Obote's.

The greatest opposition to Obote came from Buganda. The Baganda remembered Obote's deportation of Mutesa II. In retaliation for Buganda's opposition, Obote ordered mass murders in an area of Buganda north of Kampala, the Luwero Triangle. The executions in this area between 1981 and 1984 were as horrendous as any carried on under Idi Amin. The countryside throughout Luwero was littered with the remains of thousands of Obote's victims. Amnesty International estimated that between two hundred thousand and five hundred thousand Ugandans lost their lives at the hands of Obote's Uganda National Liberation Army.

Through his persecution of southern Ugandans, Obote continued the hurtful tradition of intertribal warfare that had jeopardized Uganda's national unity since the beginning. In addition to the massacre of the Baganda, Obote also attacked people in the northern districts where Amin's tribesmen and their allies lived. It has been estimated that one million Ugandans were forced to flee from this area. Meanwhile, Obote staffed the army with his own tribesmen.

Graffiti scrawled on a wall in Kampala vividly illustrated the depth of intertribal hostility. One message read: "A good Muganda is a dead Muganda. Shoot to Kill Muganda." It was signed the "Soroti Boys," a group of Obote supporters from the northern Iteso tribe.

With the leader of the country fostering warfare among Ugandans, the hopes for a unified, democratic nation dimmed. The economy continued to decline. In the first year of Obote's rule, the gross national product fell by more than it had during Amin's whole tenure. By 1984, the Ugandan shilling was valued at 350 per U.S. dollar; it had been valued at 80 to 1 in 1981. Terror, bloodshed, economic chaos, and military rule seemed to be standard issue for modern Uganda, no matter who ruled the nation.

As a military dictator, Obote faced the same threat in his second presidency that he had faced in his first—that one of his army commanders would garner enough personal support to overthrow him. This had happened with Idi Amin in 1971. It happened again in 1985. Basilio Olaro Okello, an Acholi brigadier, led an Acholi revolt within the army. Obote was defeated and exiled. Okello brought tribalism to new extremes, and there were riots in Kampala. Then, in January 1986, a new leader, Yoweri Museveni, captured the capital city, and arrived at a compromise with Okello.

Museveni had fought Obote since 1980. A member of the small western Bantu tribe, the Bahima, Museveni is an economist and scholar who was educated at University College in Dar es Salaam, Tanzania. Museveni urged cooperation among the various tribes. He maintained, "We are fighting for the democratic rights and human dignity of our peoples." He supported no faction above another. As one of his chief aides, Gertrude Njuba, explained, "Anyone who tries to lead on the basis of tribe or religion is an enemy of the people."

Museveni had headed the Uganda People's Movement, a political group that opposed Obote in the 1980 election. When Obote won, Museveni had fled to the backcountry where he organized a resistance movement called the National Resistance Movement (NRM). Museveni's guerrillas took in orphans whose parents had been murdered by Obote's troops. These "kadogas" (little ones) were an important part of NRM.

In May 1984, Obote's troops killed one hundred civilians, including an Anglican priest, in the village of Namugongo. World opinion, led by the United States, once again turned against a Ugandan head of state. Museveni's guerrillas gained new support, which continued to grow until the successful ouster of Obote and the cease-fire agreement reached by Museveni and Okello at the end of 1985.

After several months' negotiations, mediated by the president of Kenya, Daniel arap Moi, elections were held. Museveni became president of Uganda. He agreed to include representatives of all the Ugandan tribes and political parties in his government—except for Obote's Uganda National Liberation Front. The heir to the throne of Buganda, Prince Ronnie Mutebi, returned to his homeland after twenty years of exile. Museveni announced that he was willing to consider the restoration of the monarchy as a cultural symbol.

The tasks facing Museveni and the fifteen million citizens of Uganda in 1987 were formidable. In the fifteen years since independence, Uganda had sustained civil war, war with Tanzania, years of corrupt government, the deaths or dislocation of more than a million citizens, and the exile of hundreds of thousands more. The roads, public utilities, railroads, educational system, and health facilities were decimated. The foreign debt stood at $1 billion.

In his first weeks in office, Museveni declared that he would allow all groups to share power in the new government. In addition, he announced an economic plan whose goals were to increase exports and shut down the black mar-

ket. He set a curfew in Kampala and limited the power of the army to act as a police force. Soldiers were ordered to account for every bullet fired.

In spite of these plans, opposition to Museveni was constant and, at times, violent. A plot to assassinate the president involved three cabinet members. Rebel troops in the northern area of Gulu and Kitgum mounted anti-Museveni demonstrations that Museveni claimed were supported by Sudan. At the same time, tensions arose between Uganda and Kenya. In order for Museveni's economic plan to work, he had to be able to export coffee through Kenyan ports, especially Mombasa.

In Uganda, the three strongest political groups opposing Museveni are the Uganda People's Democratic Movement under Otema Allemadi, the United National Front under William Omario Lo-Arapia, and the Federal Democratic Movement under the leadership of Samuel Luwero.

A popular, though less well-organized opposition group splintered off the UPDA and fol-

Uganda's present leader,
Yoweri Museveni, member
of a small western Bantu
tribe, the Bahima, is an
economist and scholar.

lows the spiritual teachings of Alice Aluma, an Acholi herbalist. This movement blends Christianity, witchcraft, puritanism, and sadism. Aluma's two thousand followers believe that a spirit named Lakwena and several other spirits speak through her and have ordered more war to kill all the evil spirits within Uganda. And, of course, Milton Obote is still alive and undoubtedly planning a comeback. Issues dividing the country are whether to attack its economic problems with a capitalist, socialist, or communist system, and which foreign allies to support. Museveni is viewed by some as far too left of center, and he was highly criticized for inviting Amin's old ally, Muammur Qaddafy, for a state visit to Uganda.

In spite of Museveni's best intentions to unite his country peacefully, many Ugandans fear that this goal is unattainable. An Acholi woman in Gulu told a newspaper reporter, "We pregnant women do not want to have male children. We know they will die."

Even if Museveni is able to bring political and economic stability to Uganda, and even if he is able to end the nations's civil warfare, he faces yet another challenge that threatens the nation's existence. Uganda is in the throes of a medical crisis more serious than the sleeping sickness epidemic at the turn of the century. A great number of Ugandans suffer from AIDS.

Uganda is one of a number of African nations where AIDS had become epidemic. (Others

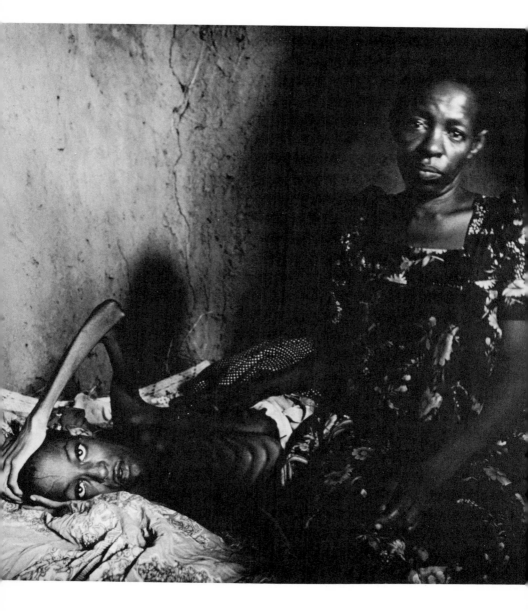

A man with AIDS being cared for by his mother

include Rwanda, Burundi, Tanzania, Zaire, and Zambia.) AIDS is a relatively new disease. The first official diagnosis of it in Uganda was made in 1984 in the Rakai District. However, scientists have thawed some Ugandan blood samples from the early 1970s and have found the critical HIV factor in as many as two-thirds of the vials. In fact, scientists at the U.S. National Cancer Institute believe AIDS originated in the area around Lake Victoria.

In Uganda, AIDS victims do not fit the profile of AIDS victims in Europe or the United States. Ugandans with AIDS are not typically homosexual, bisexual, or intravenous drug users. They are instead heterosexual, and the disease strikes women as often as it does men. The disease is called "slim disease" because of its wasting effect on its victims. Estimates of the numbers of Ugandans infected with AIDS range from 12 percent to 40 percent. Louis Ochero, head of AIDS education for Uganda, has said, "It is a disaster . . . we could lose the entire generation [people eighteen to forty] unless something drastic is done about it."

One thing that must be done is the education of Ugandans about safe sexual practices. Uganda has long been a country with a population that suffered in large numbers from sexually transmitted diseases. In the tribes, polygamy was common, and leaders from the kabaka to Idi Amin set standards of multiple wives that were emulated by the men of the country. To have numerous sexual partners has never been socially taboo in Uganda, in spite of the best efforts of the Christian missionaries. The pattern of multiple partners has led to increased incidence of venereal disease. Scientists have found that populations susceptible to venereal disease are especially susceptible to AIDS.

For Uganda, the presence of the AIDS virus in epidemic proportion is even more challenging to the medical community than it is in the United States or Europe. For Uganda must fight AIDS with a medical system that has been destroyed by the past two decades of war. The shortage of doctors, hospitals, and medicine makes the treatment of AIDS, always a difficult prospect, nearly impossible in Uganda. An AIDS test costs only $1.75, yet that small amount represents the average per capita expenditure Uganda can afford for health care.

By any measurement, the political, social and economic problems facing Uganda are enormous. The history of modern Uganda is grim; warfare, bloodshed, disease, and poverty have prevailed for almost three decades. Yet the history of Uganda before 1962 provides a different legacy for the nation. Productive agriculture, efficient governments, and a rich culture are also aspects of Uganda's heritage. Uganda's leaders must value the resources of their land and people, not destroy them, in order to provide their nation with a stable future.

GLOSSARY

Baganda—Bantu term for people living in Buganda; synonymous with *Ganda*.

Bantu—Major language group to which people in Uganda belong; Bantu tribes include the Ganda, Gisa, Sogo, Nyoro, Nkole, and Toro.

Buganda—Bantu term for land of the Ganda; kingdom on Lake Victoria, c. 1600 to the present.

Bunyoro—Bantu kingdom that rivaled Buganda for control of the area around Lake Victoria; province in modern Uganda.

Dukawallahs—Swahili term for Asian shopkeepers living in Uganda.

Gabunga—Lord high admiral in the kingdom of Buganda.

Idi Amin Dada—Military dictator of Uganda, 1971 to 1979.

Kabaka—Bantu term for king.

Karamojong—Hamitic, cattle-keeping tribe in Uganda that has clung to traditional ways.

Katikiro—Prime minister in the kingdom of Buganda.

Kitara—Name of Bantu kingdom on Lake Victoria before the Lwo invasion.

Lubareism—Religion practiced by the Bantu in Buganda before the introduction of Islam and Christianity; still practiced by a small percentage of Ugandans.

Lubuga—Queen-sister of the kabaka in a Bantu kingdom.

Lukiko—Bantu council of chiefs that acts as a legislative body.

Lwo—Nilotic people who settled near Lake Victoria in the fifteenth and sixteenth centuries.

Muganda—Bantu term for a single member of the Ganda.

Mujasi—Chief field marshal in the kingdom of Buganda.

Mukajunga—Lord high executioner in the kingdom of Buganda.

Mutesa I—Powerful king of Buganda who ruled from 1854 to 1884.

Mutesa II—Known as King Freddy; last Ganda king to rule Buganda.

Namasole—Dowager queen in the kingdom of Buganda.

Nilo-Hamitic—One of the major language groups to which people in Uganda belong; includes tribes such as the Teso, Karamojong, and Sebei.

Nilotic—One of the major language groups to which people in Uganda belong; includes tribes such as the Acholi, Alur, and Langi.

Apollo Milton Obote—Military dictator of Uganda in the late 1960s and again in the early 1980s.

Omuwanika—Treasurer of Uganda.

Rift valley—Valley formed by folding action of the earth's crust; predominant geological feature of Uganda.

Sudanese—One of the major language groups to which people in Uganda belong; includes tribes such as the Lugbara, Madi, and Kakwa.

Swahili—Language used in Uganda for everyday transactions.

Trypanosomiasis—Formal name for the deadly disease commonly known as sleeping sickness.

Tsetse fly—Insect that carries disease known as sleeping sickness to humans and cattle.

INDEX

Page numbers in *italics* refer to illustrations.

Abu Sand, 52
Acholi tribe, 35, 36, 37, 52, 69, 94, 97, 98, 104, 118
Agreement of 1900, 73
Agriculture, 12–13, 23, 29–30, 36, 75–77, *76–78*, 89, 110
AIDS, 12, 118–121, *119*
Allemadi, Otema, 117
Alur tribe, 35, 37
Amin Dada, Idi, 94–110, *96*, *99*, 120
Animal life, 27–28, 71, 101
Ankole kingdom, 68, 73
Army, 39, 92, 94–95, 97–98, 100, 107, 112

Asian population, 101–103, *102*

Baganda, defined, 31
Baker, Samuel, 51–53
Bantu language group, 22, 33, 35–38
Bell, Hesketh, 76–77
Binaisa, Godfrey, 110, 112
Bionga, 53
Bito tribe, 37
British East Africa Company, 66
Buddu kingdom, 38
Buganda, defined, 31, 37
Bugisu tribe, 69
Bukedi tribe, 69
Bunyoro kingdom, 13, 37, 39, 52–53, 61, 68, 73

Burton, Richard, 48
Buruli kingdom, 38
Burundi, 120
Bushmen, 32–33
Busoga kingdom, 37, 73

Carter, Jimmy, 104
Christian Missionary Society, 55
Christianity, 12, 20, 41, 48, 50, 51, 53, 53–61
Churchill, Winston, 13, 15
Climate, 23, 26–27
Coffee, 29, 30, 78, 89, 103, 104, 110

Daudi Chwa, 72
Democratic Party (DP), 91–92
Disease, 12, 28–29, 118–121

East Africa, 15, 18
Economy, 39, 75–79, 81, 89, 91, 100–101, 103–104, 110, 112, 113, 115, 117
Education, 21, 56
Egypt, 49, 51–52
Entebbe airfield, 105

Federal Democratic Movement, 117

Gabunga (lord high admiral), 42
Ganda, defined, 31
Geography, 22–26, 24
George VI, King of England, 83
Germany, 61, 63–65, 64, 67, 82
Gisa tribe, 35

Government, 13, 20, 38–39, 42, 68, 72–74, 80, 84–87, 89, 91–92
Great Britain, 13, 46–89

Hannington, James, 60
Haya kingdom, 41
Hima tribe, 36
Hitler, Adolf, 82, 105
Human sacrifice, 46, 58

Independence, 83, 84, 88, 89–91, 90
Islam, 12, 20, 39–41, 40, 46, 50, 51, 56, 57, 60, 61
Ismail, Khedive, 51, 52
Israelis, 105–106
Iteso tribe, 35, 113

Kabaka (king), 38–39, 42, 44, 72, 73, 89
Kabaka Yekka, 91–92
Kabarega, 52, 61
Kabugurine, 53
Kadogas (orphans), 114
Kagwa, Apolo, 72, 73
Kakwa tribe, 35, 97
Kalema, 61
Kampala, 18, 19, 23, 26, 77
Karamojong tribe, 35, 44, 69–71, 70, 111
Katikiro (prime minister), 42, 72
Kawalya-Kagwa, Mikaeri, 85
Kenya, 15, 18, 26, 91, 106
Kenyatta, Jomo, 92, 93
Kigezi District, 74
Kitara kingdom, 37
Kiwewa, 61
Kulubya, Serwano, 85

Lakes, 18, 22, 26

Lake Victoria, 22–23, 32, 49
Land ownership, 73, 77, 78
Langi tribe, 35, 36, 69, 94, 97, 98, 104
Lango District, 74
Language groups, 20, 22, 33–35
Life expectancy, 20, 71
Literacy, 18
Livingstone, David, 48, 49
Lo-Arapia, William Omario, 117
Logo tribe, 35
Luba-Lunda region, 35
Lubareism, 46, 50, 61
Lubuga (queen-sister), 42
Luganda, 31
Lugard, Frederick, 66
Lugbara tribe, 35
Lukiko (parliament), 42, 72, 73, 84, 86, 87, 89, 91
Lule, Yusuf, 109–110
Luwero, Samuel, 117
Luwero Triangle, 112
Lwo tribe, 36, 37

MacKay, Alexander, 55–58
Madi tribe, 35
Mau Mau rebellion, 97
Mboya, Tom, 92
Medicine, 20, 71, 121
Middle class, 79
Mineral resources, 26
Missionaries, 41, 53–61, 54
Moi, Daniel arap, 115
Mountains, 23–26
Mountains of the Moon, 23–25, 27
Mufumbiro volcanoes, 26
Muganda, 31
Muhavura, 26

Mujasi (field marshal), 42
Mukajunga (lord high executioner), 42
Museveni, Yoweri, 114–118, *116*
Mutebi, Prince Ronnie, 115
Mutesa I, 41–43, 47, 50–53
Mutesa II, 37
Mutesa II (King Freddy), 87–89, *88*, 92, 94, 95
Mwanga, 47, 58–61, 65, 66, 72–73

Nagana, 28–29
Namasole (dowager queen), 42
Native Law Ordinance of 1919, 74
Nile River, 25, 48, 49
Nilo-Hamitic language group, 22, 34, 35
Nilotic language group, 22, 34–36
Njuba, Gertrude, 114
Nkole tribe, 35
Nsibirwa, Martin Luther, 85
Nyerere, Julius, 107
Nyoro tribe, 35

Obote, Apollo Milton, 92–95, *93*, 97–98, 107, 109, *111*–115, 118
Ochero, Louis, 120
Okello, Basilio Olaro, 113–115
Omuwanika (treasurer), 85
Organization of African Unity (OAU), 106

Political parties, 91
Political patronage, 38
Polygamy, 120

Population, 18, 91
Pre-Cambrian period, 22
Protestants, 56, 57, 59–61, 66
Proto-Hamites, 32–33

Qaddafy, Muammur, 104, 105, 118

Railroads, 76, 77
Religion, 12, 20, 41, 46, 50–51, 53–61
Rift valleys, 22
Roads, 77, 103
Roman Catholics, 56–61, 66, 92
Ruwenzori Mountains, 23–25, 24, 27
Ruwenzori National Park, 101
Rwanda, 18, 26, 120

Sangoan culture, 32
Sebei tribe, 35, 69
Slaves, 39–41, 40, 50–53
Sleeping sickness, 12, 28–29
Snay bia Amin, 41
Soga tribe, 35, 36, 41
Somali, 18
Speke, John Hanning, 41, 42, 46–50
Spheres of influence, 65, 67
Stanley, Henry Morton, 48, 53–55, 54
Stone Age, 32
Sudan, 18
Sudanic language group, 22, 34, 35
Sulaiman bin Zcher, 60
Suna, 50
Swahili language group, 22

Tanganyika, 15, 91
Tanzania, 15, 18, 26, 98, 107–108, 120
Taxation, 73, 75
Teso tribe, 69
Tools, 32, 35
Toro kingdom, 35, 68, 73
Transportation, 75–77, 80
Tribal hostility, 33, 35–38, 47–48, 112–114
Trypanosomiasis, 28–29
Tsetse fly, 28, 71
Turkana tribe, 69
Tutsi tribe, 36

Uganda National Liberation Army, 112
Uganda National Liberation Front, 110, 115
Uganda People's Congress (UPC), 91–92
Uganda People's Democratic Movement, 117
Uganda People's Movement, 114
Uganda Protectorate, 66, 68–81
Uganda Railway, 76
Uganda Rifles, 94, 97
United National Front, 117

Venereal disease, 121

Weapons, 39–41
White Fathers, 56, 57, 59
Wilson, George, 72
World War I, 83
World War II, 82–83

Zaire, 18, 26, 35, 120
Zambia, 120
Zanzibar, 15, 91
Zanzibari traders, 39–41, 40, 50–53, 60